World Class

EXPANDING ENGLISH FLUENCY

NANCY DOUGLAS | JAMES R. MORGAN

NATIONAL GEOGRAPHIC LEARNING

CENGAGE Learning·

Australia • Brazil • Japan • Korea • Mexico • Singapore • Spain • United Kingdom • United States

**World Class: Expanding English Fluency
Student Edition**

Nancy Douglas and James R. Morgan

Publisher: Sherrise Roehr

Managing Editor: Sarah Thérèse Kenney

Development Editors: Michael Poor, Michael Tom

Senior Technology Product Manager: Scott Rule

Technology Project Manager: Chris Conroy

Director of Global Marketing: Ian Martin

Senior Product Marketing Manager: Katie Kelley

Director, Content and Media Production:
Michael Burggren

Content Project Manager: Andrea Bobotas

Print Buyer: Mary Beth Hennebury

Cover Designer: Cenveo Publisher Services

Cover Image: Jeff Curtes

Compositor: Cenveo Publisher Services

For product information and technology assistance, contact us at
**Cengage Learning Customer & Sales Support,
1-800-354-9706**

For permission to use material from this text or product,
submit all requests online at **www.cengage.com/permissions.**
Further permissions questions can be e-mailed to
permissionrequest@cengage.com.

Student Book + Student CD-ROM ISBN: 978-1-133-31081-5

Student Book + Online Workbook ISBN: 978-1-285-06309-6

National Geographic Learning
20 Channel Center Street
Boston, MA 02210
USA

Cengage Learning is a leading provider of customized learning solutions with office locations around the globe, including Singapore, the United Kingdom, Australia, Mexico, Brazil and Japan.

Cengage Learning products are represented in Canada by Nelson Education, Ltd.

Visit National Geographic Learning online at **ngl.cengage.com**

Visit our corporate website at **www.cengage.com**

Printed in the United States of America
1 2 3 4 5 6 7 8 9 10   15 14 13 12

Acknowledgements

The authors and editorial team would like to thank the many dedicated instructors who took the time to review World Class. *Their feedback was invaluable during the development of this program.*

UNITED STATES Touria Ghaffari, EC New York, New York, New York; **Olga Gusak,** Computer Systems Institute, Skokie, Illinois; **William Jex,** American Language Institute, New York University, New York, New York; **Bridget McDonald,** Independent Learning Services, Boston, Massachusetts; **Saida Pagan,** North Valley OC, Mission Hills, California; **Tara Tarpey,** American Language Institute, New York University, New York, New York

LATIN AMERICA Luiz Otávio Barros, Associação Alumni, Brazil; **Clarissa Bezerra,** Casa Thomas Jefferson, Brazil; **Isabela Villas Boas,** Casa Thomas Jefferson, Brazil; **Tatiane C. de Carvalho,** Cultura Britânica e Americana, Brazil; **Rafael Reis Carpanez,** Cultura Inglesa, Brazil; **Janette Carvalhinho de Oliveira,** Centro de Linguas - UFES, Brazil; **Samara Camilo Tomé Costa,** IBEU, Brazil; **Frank Couto,** Casa Thomas Jefferson, Brazil; **Denise Santos da Silva,** Associação Cultural Estados Unidos, Brazil; **Marilena Fernandes,** Associação Alumni, Brazil; **Vanessa Ferreira,** Associação Cultural Brasil Estados Unidos, Brazil; **Marcia Ferreira,** CCBEU Franca, Brazil; **Maria Regina Filgueiras,** College Language Center, Brazil; **Maria Righini,** Associação Cultura Inglesa, Brazil; **Bebeth Silva Costa,** Betina's English Course, Brazil; **Domingos Sávio Siqueira,** Federal University of Bahia, Brazil; **Joyce von Söhsten,** English by Joyce von Söhsten, Brazil; **Doris Flores,** Universidad Santo Tomas, Chile; **Sandra Herrera,** Inacap Apoquindo, Chile; **Jair Ayala Zarate,** La Salle University, Colombia; **Rosario Mena,** Instituto Cultural Dominico Americano, Dominican Republic; **Raúl Billini,** Language Program Administration, Dominican Republic; **Rosa Vásquez,** John F. Kennedy Institute of Languages, INC., Dominican Republic; **Elizabeth Ortiz,** COPEI-COPOL English Institute, Ecuador; **José Alonso Gaxiola Soto,** Universidad Autonoma de Sinaloa, Mexico; **María Elena Mesías Ratto,** Universidad de San Martín de Porres, Peru

EUROPE AND THE MIDDLE EAST Juan Irigoyen, International Institute, Spain; **Nashwa Nashaat Sobhy,** San Jorge University, Spain; **Barbara Van der Veer,** International Institute, Spain **Deborah Wilson,** American University of Sharjah, United Arab Emirates

ASIA Michael Lay, American Intercon Institute, Cambodia; **Kirkland Arizona Kenney,** Beijing New Oriental School, China; **Isao Akama,** Waseda University, Japan; **Benjamin Bailey,** University of Shizuoka, Japan; **James Baldwin,** Toyko University of Agriculture and Technology, Japan; **Jonathan deHaan,** University of Shizuoka, Japan; **Todd Enslen,** Tohoku University, Japan; **Peter Gray,** Hokusei Gakuen University, Japan; **Linda Hausman,** Gakushuin University, Japan; **Mauro Lo Dico,** Nanzan University, Japan; **Nobue Mori,** Kumamoto Gakuen University, Japan; **Yuri Nishio,** Gifu Pharmaceutical University, Japan; **Geraldine Norris,** The Prefectual University of Shizuoka, Japan; **Christopher Piper,** Takushoku University, Japan; **Michael Radcliffe,** Yokohama City University, Japan; **Jean-Pierre Richard,** Kanagawa University, Sophia University, Japan; **Greg Rouault,** Konan University, Hirao School of Management, Japan; **Stephen Ryan,** Yamagata University, Japan; **Gregory Strong,** Aoyama Gakuin University, Japan; **Michael Yasui,** Tokyo Metropolitan University, Japan; **Sun Mi Ma,** Ajou University, Korea; **Palarak Chaiyo,** Rajamangala University of Technology Suvarnabhumi, Thailand; **Krishna Kosashunhanan,** Thai-Nichai Institute of Technology, Thailand; **Jonee de Leon,** Universal English Center, Vietnam; **Ai Nguyen Huynh Thi,** VUS, Vietnam

We would also like to extend a special thank-you to Yeny Kim for her many insights. Her thoughtful contributions were a great asset and will be felt by students and teachers alike.

UNIT	VOCABULARY	GRAMMAR	LISTENING
UNIT 1 Who Are We?, 1	Who is the world's most typical human?	Review of Past Tense	New Family Tree website **Pronunciation:** Rising and falling intonation
UNIT 2 The World Awaits, 12	Popular vacation destinations **Pronunciation:** Stress changes with prefixes and suffixes	Uses of Infinitives and Gerunds	A walking tour of Bejing
UNIT 3 The Great Energy Challenge, 24	An energy quiz **Pronunciation:** Heteronyms and stress shift	Review of Future Forms	The family energy challenge
UNIT 4 The World's a Stage, 36	The story of Esmee Denters, Youtube sensation	Infinitive Complements (*persuade* verbs, *want* verbs, *believe* verbs, and *make* verbs)	Interview with a salsa band musician
UNIT 5 No Need to Panic, 48	People who have beat the odds	Adverbial Clauses	There is no need to panic
UNIT 6 In Style, 60	The Dubai Shopping Festival	Adjective Clauses with Subject Relative Pronouns **Pronunciation:** Intonation patterns in relative clauses	Conversations at a shopping mall

READING	WRITING	SPEAKING	VIDEO
Cleopatra: The Search for the Last Queen of Egypt	Write a personal statement as part of an application **Strategy:** Writing a personal statement	Interview to be a cultural ambassador **Strategy:** Responding to questions	*The Human Family Tree*
Traveling Troubadour: An interview with singer Jason Mraz	Write a descriptive paragraph about a place **Strategy:** Create a mental image	Create a bucket list of things you want to do **Strategy:** Making suggestions and giving advice	*Barcelona's Street Life*
Plugging Into the Sun: Why don't we use solar energy more? **Strategy:** Identifying key details	Write a persuasive paragraph that presents and justifies your point of view **Strategy:** Being persuasive	Persuade an audience to make a change	*We Need to Be Leaders Ourselves*
Hip Hop Goes Home: A struggling rapper in Africa	Write a profile of a person that you admire **Strategy:** Paraphrasing	Analyzing a music contract **Strategy:** Talking pros and cons	*Songs under a Big Sky* (excerpt): Profile of Irish singer Iarla Ó Lionáird
Everest's Deadliest Day: Two teams compete to reach the summit first – with deadly results	Write a set of instructions describing how to do something **Strategy:** Explaining the steps in a process	Discuss a difficult environmental issue **Strategy:** Reaching a compromise	*Surviving Deadly Everest*
Every Shoe Tells a Story: They say a lot about us, even when we're not wearing them	Present and defend and argument **Strategy:** Making a successful argument	Give your opinions in a shopping and fashion survey **Strategy:** Reacting to someone else's point of view	*How to Spot a Fake Louis Vuitton Bag*

READING	WRITING	SPEAKING	VIDEO
One Foot on The Gas: Children of immigrants discover American car culture	Write a letter of complaint	Consider the facts in an immigration case **Strategy:** Presenting facts and announcing a decision	*Capital Bikeshare*
Nowhere to Hide: What happens when our private lives become public	Give an opinion on an event **Strategy:** Writing an effective online post	Evaluate different surveillance practices	*Protecting reputations online*
Orphan Elephants: A center in Kenya rescues, rehabilitates and researches baby elephants	Write an informational brochure **Strategy:** Getting the reader's attention	Debate what to do about three animals at risk	*Great Migrations* (excerpt)
The Teenage Brain: Why teenagers act the way they do **Strategy:** Recognizing cause and effect	Use cause and effect to explain a decision you'd make **Strategy:** Showing cause and effect	Analyze how you handle peer pressure	*Moral Dilemma* (excerpt): **Pronunciation:** Thought groups
Storm Chasers: Scientists risk their lives to gather data about tornadoes **Strategy:** Making inferences	Describe a time weather impacted your life **Strategy:** Include figurative language	Which weather story is false?	*Sinking England*
The Spirit of Kung Fu: A Shaolin master faces the world of kung fu	Write about important qualities **Strategy:** Writing a timed essay	Present an activity **Strategy:** Speaking from an outline	Alain Robert, *"The French Spiderman"*

Explore a Unit

The first half of each unit leads students through guided and communicative practice to master target structures.

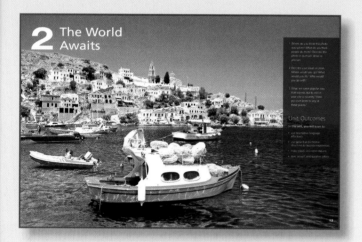

Clearly stated **Unit Outcomes** provide a roadmap of learning for the student.

Stunning images and thought-provoking questions encourage learners to **think critically** about the unit theme.

Relevant, high frequency vocabulary is practiced in contextualized exercises.

Pronunciation boxes offer support and tips as well as cross reference to full explanation and practice in the appendix.

The **Grammar** section allows learners to refine their grammar skills and practice the grammar through first controlled and then open-ended activities.

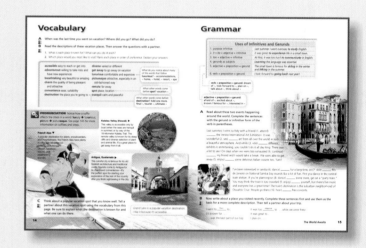

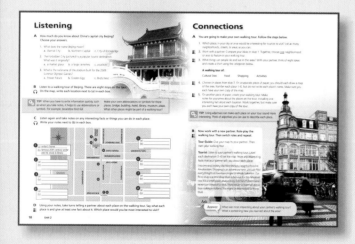

Listening activities encourage learners to listen for and consolidate key information, reinforcing the language, and allowing learners to personalize and think critically about the information they hear.

The **Connections** section allows learners to synthesize the vocabulary and grammar they have learned through personalized communication.

The second half of the unit focuses on skill-building and communication. The strands build on one another with a final communicative task before Expanding Your Fluency. For this reason, the order of strands may vary from unit to unit.

Learners navigate **interesting and relevant readings** from National Geographic through pre-, while-, and post-reading activities, helping them to comprehend the main idea and key details of the passage.

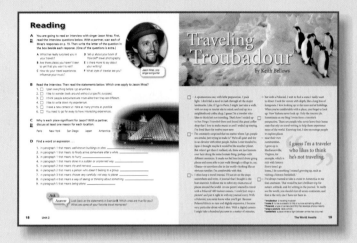

Learners are encouraged to perform **Speaking** tasks in pairs and groups. Where appropriate, **strategies** are provided to ensure students' successful communication.

The **Video** section brings the world into the classroom with authentic clips, including news stories, PSAs, and National Geographic documentaries.

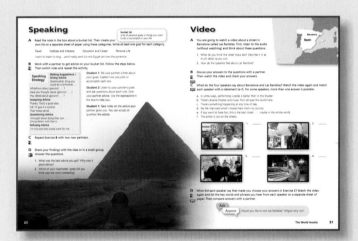

The **Writing** section includes writing models to prompt learners to complete a functional piece of writing and also serves as a culminating activity in many units.

The **Expanding Your Fluency** section allows learners to apply the language they have learned throughout the unit in real-world tasks and offers self-assessment checks.

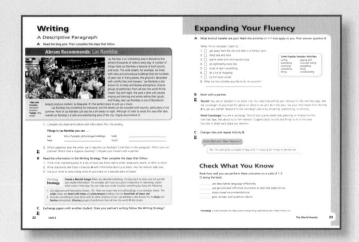

1 Who We Are

1 Look at the four photos. Who are these people? Describe each person in as much detail as you can.

2 Where do you think these people come from? Tell a story about one of them.

3 Do you think you have anything in common with the people in the photos? Why or why not?

Unit Outcomes

In this unit, you will learn to:

- use past tenses to ask and answer questions about memorable life events

- summarize the key outcomes of a study

- explain and evaluate qualifications

- handle challenging questions

Vocabulary

A Describe the most typical person at your school. Do you fit the description of the "most typical person"? Why or why not? Tell a partner.

> The typical person in this school is between 19 and 22 years old, has dark hair . . .

ambitious needing exceptional effort and resources to be carried out successfully; the desire to achieve something exceptional

average the normal amount or quality for a group of things or people

come up with to suggest or think of an idea or plan

> **average** ~ year, ~ day, ~ income, above/below ~

determine to find out or to confirm certain information

set out to start trying to do something

statistics numerical facts that are gathered through analyzing information

trait a particular characteristic a person has

typical showing the most usual characteristics of a person or thing

> **typical** ~ day, ~ student, ~ pattern, ~ behavior

B On our planet of seven billion people, who is the most typical human? In an ambitious effort, scientists set out to list the traits of the most typical human being. Guess what they found.

According to statistics, the average person . . .

1. speaks   Spanish / English / Chinese / French.
2. is   male / female.
3. is   under 20 / 21–30 / over 30.
4. has / doesn't have   a cell phone.
5. has / doesn't have   a bank account.
6. lives   in a big city / in a small suburb / in the country.

C To determine what the average human being on Earth looks like, scientists then collected photos of 190,000 of the world's most typical people. After combining the photos electronically, the scientists came up with a face that looked like one of the photos on the unit opener. In pairs, discuss: Which photo is it?

> Ask
>
> Answer   How similar are you to the world's most typical person? Explain your answer with examples.

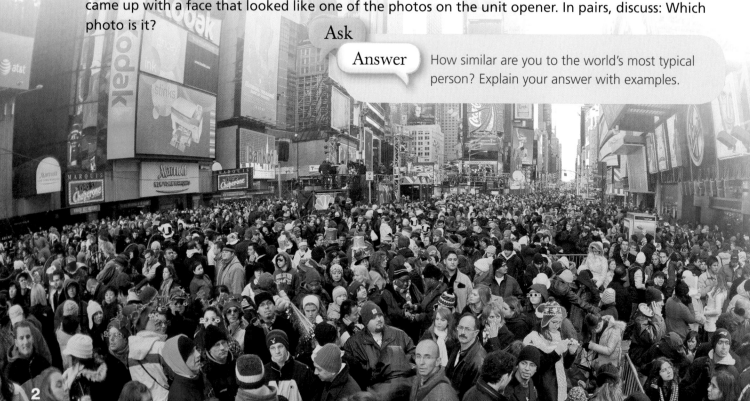

Grammar

A What do we know about Dan's living situation? Match each sentence (1–4) with an explanation (a–c).
Use the chart to help you. Explain your answers to a partner.

1. Dan lived in Europe for two years.
2. Dan was living in Europe at the time.

3. Dan has lived in Europe since 2010.
4. Dan has been living in Europe for two years.

a. Dan lives in Europe now.
b. Dan doesn't live in Europe anymore.
c. Dan may or may not live in Europe now.

TIP Use *for* (+ a period of time) and *since* (+ a specific point in time) with the perfect tenses to describe "time up to now." Use *for* (but not *since*) with the simple past tense for a time period that has come to an end.

Review of Past Tenses

simple past: Use for actions completed in the past at a specific time (sometimes inferred). Use time expressions like *a year ago, earlier today, last summer,* and *the other day*.	We **graduated** together.
	He **worked** there for a year.
past continuous: Use for ongoing past actions that may or may not be completed. Use with the simple past to describe what was going on when the action in the simple past occurred.	I **was working** all day yesterday.
	We **were studying** in college when we rented that apartment.
present perfect: Use for actions begun in the past and continuing up to now and for actions in the past that relate to the present. Use time expressions like *lately, recently, up to now, during the last two months,* and *this week*.	I've **worked** here for a year.
	Have you ever **studied** Portuguese?
present perfect continuous: Use to emphasize the length of an event. In spoken English the verb *to be* is almost always a contraction.	Recently, I've **been working** too much.
	She's **been waiting** for an hour!

B Read about Liam. Complete each sentence with the correct past form of the verb in parentheses.

During and after college He (1. live) _____ in the dorms while he (2. attend) _____ college. After graduation, he (3. move) _____ back in with his parents for a year to save money. He (4. live) _____ there ever since.

Occupation He (5. start) _____ a small business with two other people when he (6. be) _____ 24. It (7. close) _____ a year ago. Since then, he (8. work) _____ for a large tech company.

Health He never (9. smoke) _____ in his life. Last year, he (10. run) _____ in his first marathon.

Relationships He (11. meet) _____ his wife two years ago. They (12. talk) _____ about having a baby in the next year.

> Where did he live while he was attending college?

C Now ask your partner three questions about Liam.

D Now it's your turn! In pairs, tell each other a little bit about yourselves, using the same categories and model language in Activity **B**.

Listening

A Look at the illustration. Answer the questions with a partner.

1. What do you know about your family tree? Tell your partner two facts.
2. How did you learn that information? How has your family history been preserved?

B Listen to an advertisement for a Web site. Mark all of the statements that are true.

New Family Tree . . .

☐ focuses on family statistics and research.

☐ lets you upload photos and video.

☐ connects you with families all over the world.

☐ allows members to share and tell stories.

☐ enables you to share memories with your relatives.

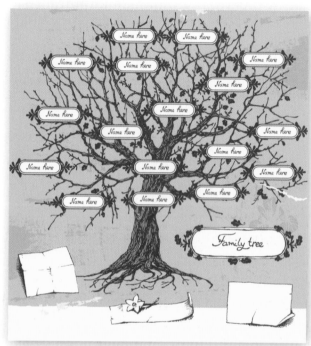

A family tree is a diagram that shows family members and their relationships over several generations. Typically, the older generations are at the top of the tree and the youngest relatives are at the bottom.

TIP Listen for words or ideas that are repeated. Repeated information often means that it is important and you should pay attention.

C How does the site work? Listen and number the steps in the correct order. One step is extra.

_____ a. choose a question

_____ b. send the question to someone

_____ c. log in

_____ d. pay a membership fee

_____ e. write an answer to the question

_____ f. read the answer to the question

PRONUNCIATION Notice that the pitch of your voice should drop at the end of these questions. See page 144 for more information on intonation.

D What kinds of questions can you answer on the site? Listen again and complete the sample questions below. Then choose one and ask your partner about it.

1. How did you
   _____?

2. Who was your
   _____?

3. What's your favorite
   _____?

4. Have you ever
   _____?

5. What is a memory from your childhood that
   _____?

Video

A You are going to watch the video *The Human Family Tree*. Complete the sentences with the correct options.

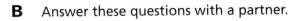

ancestors	determine	generations	setting out

Scientists are (1) _____ to answer some questions. On a single street in New York City, they are collecting DNA samples from people from all over the world including Thailand, Ecuador, Africa, and the Caribbean. They are trying to use the DNA to come up with some answers about the past. Will the scientists be able to use the samples to trace back each person's (2) _____ many (3) _____ and (4) _____ where they came from? And will they learn anything about the "human family tree"?

DNA, the building blocks of life.

B Answer these questions with a partner.

1. Why are the scientists doing DNA tests in New York City?
2. What do you think they will learn about the "human family tree"?

C Watch the video. Decide if each statement is true or false. Then, correct the false sentences to make them true. Explain your answers to a partner.

1. A key human question is: "Where are my ancestors?"	True	False
2. Typically, we can trace our family tree back one or two generations.	True	False
3. DNA testing takes us back up to twelve generations.	True	False
4. We each carry a kind of genetic historic document inside us.	True	False
5. Our ancestors adapted to different cultures.	True	False
6. At the genetic level, we are basically identical.	True	False

> **⚙ VIDEO GLOSSARY**
>
> **adapt** to change your ideas or behavior to suit a different situation
>
> **genetics** the study of how certain characteristics (e.g., eye color, hair color, and skin color) are passed from one generation to the next by our genes
>
> **identical** exactly the same

D Summarize the video in your own words. Use these questions to help you.

What was happening?
Who was leading the study, and why did they do it?
What did they discover?
What were people hoping to find out?

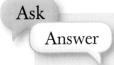

Would you be interested in participating in this study? Why or why not?

Reading

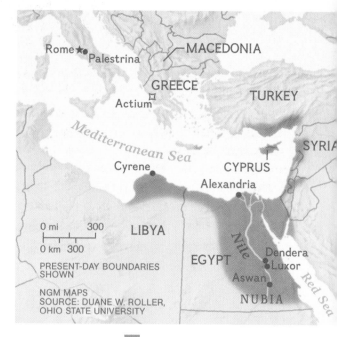

PRESENT-DAY BOUNDARIES SHOWN

NGM MAPS
SOURCE: DUANE W. ROLLER,
OHIO STATE UNIVERSITY

■ Cleopatra's kingdom at greatest extent, 34–31 B.C.

A Read the title of the passage and look at the photos. With a partner, make a list of everything you know about Cleopatra. Then read the passage. How many of your ideas were mentioned in the article?

B Next to each statement, write the correct letter (*T, F,* or *P*). Underline the information in the passage that helped you choose your answers.

> **T** = definitely true   **P** = possible, but not 100% certain
> **F** = definitely false

Cleopatra . . .

_____ 1. was Egypt's first queen.

_____ 2. was Greek.

_____ 3. was well-educated.

_____ 4. was a beautiful woman.

_____ 5. had four children.

_____ 6. was killed by a snake.

_____ 7. was honored by the Romans after her death.

_____ 8. is buried near the city of Alexandria.

C Why are these numbers and dates important to Cleopatra's life and the search for her? Write your answers on another piece of paper.

| 69 BCE | 4 | 18 | 22 | 44 BCE | 30 BCE | 39 | 20,000 |

D Use the information in Exercises **B** and **C** to summarize Cleopatra's life.

E Make a list of 4–6 ages, numbers, and dates that are important in your life. Use them to tell a partner about "who you are."

F It's time to step out of your own identity and into someone else's. Get into a small group of 3–5 people. One person is a TV talk show host who interviews popular celebrities. The others are today's guests on the show; you can choose from Cleopatra, her brother Ptolemy, Julius Caesar, and Marc Antony. You are going to create a 2–3 minute role-play.

- First, come up with 5–6 interesting questions to ask the show's guests. Decide how each guest would respond. Use information from the reading and your imaginations to help you.
- Present your role-play to another group.

Ask

Answer   What do you think of Cleopatra? Do you admire her?

The deadly snake sat in its case. "Bring me the basket!" Cleopatra ordered her servants. Roman soldiers were invading[1] her country, and the queen of Egypt would rather die than live as a prisoner. Cleopatra picked up the snake and let it bite her. Within minutes, she was dead.

This story has been told for centuries. But did it really happen? Like so much about Cleopatra, no one knows for sure.

Teen Queen

We know little about Cleopatra, but some information about her has survived. We know, for example, that she was born in 69 BCE to a Greek family who ruled Egypt for nearly three hundred years. Growing up in Alexandria, Cleopatra studied science and math. She also learned to speak several languages, including Greek, Latin, and Egyptian.

Cleopatra (left) in one of the few images that still exists of her.

By the time she became queen at age 18, Egypt—one of the world's richest nations—was in trouble. The Roman Empire was planning to invade. Cleopatra was also at war with her younger brother, Ptolemy. To stop him, Cleopatra persuaded[2] the Roman general Julius Caesar to help her. With Caesar's help, Cleopatra defeated[3] her brother. Caesar also helped Cleopatra preserve Egypt's independence from Rome.

The partners soon became a couple, and at age 22, Cleopatra had a son. After Caesar's death in 44 BCE, Cleopatra met another powerful Roman, Marc Antony. The pair eventually had three children, and for years they fought to stop Rome from invading Egypt. In the summer of 30 BCE, though, Rome won. Rather than accept defeat, Marc Antony and Cleopatra killed themselves. Cleopatra—Egypt's last pharaoh (ruler)—was 39 years old.

Erasing the Past

After Cleopatra died, the Romans invented negative stories about her and destroyed art with her image on it. They didn't want Egyptians to remember their former queen. Over time, earthquakes also destroyed buildings, and the sea around Alexandria rose. Within a few hundred years, most of Cleopatra's world was buried[4] under water. As a result, we know very little about how Cleopatra lived or exactly how she died. Although stories often describe her as beautiful, we don't really know what she looked like.

The Search Begins

But this may be changing. Today, archaeologists[5] have started searching the Mediterranean near Alexandria, Cleopatra's home. So far, they've brought up 20,000 objects from the sea. Many probably existed during Cleopatra's lifetime.

On land nearby, other archaeologists have discovered new tombs, and there are signs that someone important may be buried there. "My dream is to find a statue of Cleopatra," says one explorer. So far, however, neither search has located Cleopatra—yet.

---

[1] **invading** entering a country by force with an army
[2] **persuade** to cause someone to do something by giving good reasons for doing it
[3] **defeat** to win a victory over someone in a battle or game
[4] **buried** under the ground and covered with earth
[5] **archaeologists** scientists who study people and societies of the past

Connections

A Read the ad. Then discuss with a partner: What does a cultural ambassador do? What personality traits should a good cultural ambassador have?

Be a cultural ambassador in Australia!

Australia Cultural Exchange (ACEX) is a three-month program for people who want to improve their English, learn about another culture, and teach others about their own. Individuals in the program act as cultural ambassadors. As a representative of your country, you will travel around Australia and visit local schools. You'll talk to others about your country and customs. For more information and to fill out your application, visit www.ACEX.au.ng.

B You are applying for this position. Complete Sections 1–4 (not 5) of the application.

AUSTRALIA CULTURAL EXCHANGE

SECTION 1: STUDENT INFORMATION

Name (first, middle, last)

Date of birth   E-mail address

City   State/Territory   Country

SECTION 2: EDUCATION

School	Location	Dates attended	Major

SECTION 3: LANGUAGES AND TRAVEL EXPERIENCE

Languages you speak   Years studied

Travel experience (domestic or international)

SECTION 4: ACTIVITIES

Please list any activities that you participate in: work, sports, music, etc.

Activity	Years/months doing it	Hours each week	Awards won

SECTION 5: PERSONAL STATEMENT

Why do you want to be a cultural ambassador? Why would you be a good one? Explain which personal traits, education, skills, and experience you have.

C Take turns. Tell a partner at least one thing about yourself from each of the first four sections of the application. Then join another pair of students and introduce your partner to them.

Writing
A Personal Statement

A Read one student's personal statement and answer the questions.

Writing
Strategy

Writing a Personal Statement
Before you write, read the information about the school or company. What qualities are they looking for in an applicant? Next, write down the facts about your personal experience. Finally, write your statement and show how your background makes you the kind of person they are seeking. Pay attention to the use of past tenses.

> I want to be a cultural ambassador because I'm interested in learning more about Australia. I also want to teach others about my country, Brazil. I believe that my background and experience have prepared me to participate in the ACEX program in different ways.
>
> To be a good cultural ambassador, a person should be knowledgeable about his culture. I think I am. For example, I've been studying capoeira for the last three years. Capoeira is a Brazilian art form that combines dance and martial arts. I practice for eight hours a week, and I love it. Once I performed for a group of tourists. After the performance, they asked many questions about capoeira and Brazil. I enjoyed telling them about both in English.
>
> I've always liked learning about other cultures, too. I majored in English, and I also speak some Spanish. I have never traveled outside Brazil, but I've met many people from all over the world here in Sao Paulo. I believe this experience has also prepared me to participate in this program.
>
> I am ready to set out on a big adventure—to be a cultural ambassador in Australia. I think it's important to learn about other countries' customs and to share your own with the rest of the world. I hope that you will consider my application!

First paragraph: Explain why you are applying.

TIP Be sure to define any words (e.g., *capoeira*) that are unfamiliar to your reader.

Last paragraph: Restate your interest in the position.

1. Did the applicant answer both questions asked in Section 5 of the application on page 8?
2. Would he be a good cultural ambassador? Why or why not?

B Now write your own personal statement.

- Reread Sections 1–4 of your application on page 8. What information is important to include in your statement?
- Look back at your list of traits in Exercise **A** on page 8. Which ones describe you? Include them in your statement.

C Exchange papers with another student. Read your partner's statement. Does it . . .

- answer both questions asked in Section 5 of the application?
- follow the Writing Strategy?

Capoeira dancer

9

Speaking

A Imagine that you work for the ACEX program. You are going to interview people who have applied to be cultural ambassadors in Australia. Read the questions below. Then look back at the application on page 8 and write six additional interview questions on a separate piece of paper. Remember: you want to learn about the applicant's background, education, skills, and activities in as much detail as you can. You also want to know why the person wants to be a cultural ambassador.

1. Tell me a little about yourself. Where are you from? Have you ever lived or traveled anywhere else?
2. What are your hobbies? How long have you been [doing that hobby]? Why did you decide to do it?

TIP Here are some useful prompts to help formulate additional questions.

- Tell me more about . . .
- Why did you decide to . . .
- What did you learn from . . .
- Why is _____ important to you?
- Have you ever . . .

B Work in pairs. One of you will interview the other, using your questions from Exercise **A**. Take notes on your partner's responses. Use the expressions in the Speaking Strategy to help you.

So, tell me: Why do you want to be a cultural ambassador?

Great question. I guess the main reason is . . .

C Switch roles and repeat Exercise **B**.

Ask

Answer Do you want to be a cultural ambassador? If so, to which country?

Speaking Strategy	**Responding to questions** It's common to get nervous in an interview, especially when you're asked a difficult question. To give yourself a little time to prepare your answer, try these strategies. Just don't overuse them!

Complimenting the interviewer for asking the question

(That's a) good / great question.
I'm glad you asked (me) that (question).

Showing your experience with the question

Actually, I've been asked that question several times. / People ask me that question a lot.
That's interesting. I've never been asked that before.

Repeating the question

Interviewer: Have you ever traveled outside your country?
Interviewee: Have I ever traveled outside my country? Well, no I haven't, but . . .

Expanding Your Fluency

Before You Play

- Work in a group of four. Complete the questions on the game board.
- Take ten small pieces of paper. Write *T* (true) on five pieces and *F* (false) on the other five. Shuffle the papers and place them face down in a deck.
- Put your markers on START.

Playing the Game

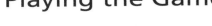Flip a coin. Heads = move one square. Tails = move two squares. Read the question on that square.

- Turn over a piece of paper; don't show your group. If the paper says *T*, answer the question truthfully. If it says *F*, make up an answer. Return the paper to the bottom of the deck.
- Each person will ask you one follow-up question to determine if you are telling the truth.
- Finally, each person guesses if it's the truth or not. If most people guess correctly, you stay where you are. If most people guess incorrectly, you move forward one space. The first player to reach FINISH is the winner!

→ 10. Have you ever (be) _____ out of the country?	11. What were you (think) _____ about when you (wake) _____ up this morning?	12. What book are you reading now and how long have you (read) _____ it?	13. Have you ever (meet) _____ a famous person? Who?	**FINISH**
↑ 9. When was the last time you (get) _____ angry?	← 8. Have you ever (buy) _____ anything expensive?	7. What (do) _____ you do on your last day off?	6. How many times have you (move) _____ in your life?	← 5. What were you (do) _____ between 6:00 and 8:00 p.m. last night?
START →	1. When was the last time you (eat) _____ something you didn't like?	2. Have you ever (visit) _____ relatives in another city?	→ 3. Who were you (sit) _____ next to in class yesterday?	↑ 4. How long have you (study) _____ English?

Check What You Know

Rank how well you can perform these outcomes on a scale of 1–5
(5 being the best).

_____ use past tenses to ask and answer questions about memorable life events

_____ summarize the key outcomes of a study

_____ explain and evaluate qualifications

_____ handle challenging questions

2 The World Awaits

1 Where do you think this photo was taken? What do you think people do there? Describe the photo in as much detail as you can.

2 Describe your ideal vacation. Where would you go? What would you do? Who would you go with?

3 What are some popular sites that tourists like to visit in your city or country? Have you ever been to any of these places?

Unit Outcomes

In this unit, you will learn to:

- use descriptive language effectively

- use gerund and infinitive structures to describe experiences

- make travel recommendations

- give, accept, and question advice

Vocabulary

A   When was the last time you went on vacation? Where did you go? What did you do?

B   Read the descriptions of these vacation places. Then answer the questions with a partner.

    1.   What is each place known for? What can you do at each?

    2.   Which place would you most like to visit? Rank each place in order of preference. Explain your answers.

accessible easy to reach or get into	**diverse** varied or different
adventurous willing to take risks and have new experiences	**get away** to go away on vacation
breathtaking very beautiful or amazing	**luxurious** comfortable and expensive
charm the quality of being pleasant and attractive	**picturesque** attractive, especially in an old-fashioned way
convenience ease; suitability	**remote** far away
destination the place you're going to	**spot** place; location
	tranquil calm and peaceful

What do you notice about many of the words that follow **luxurious**? ~ accommodations, ~ home, ~ hotel, ~ resort, ~ spa

What other words come before **spot**? vacation ~

What other words come before **destination**? Add one more. final ~, tourist ~, ultimate ~

PRONUNCIATION Notice how a suffix affects the stress in a word: **lux**ury ➜ lux**ur**ious; **pic**ture ➜ pictur**esque**. See page 145 for more information on suffixes and stress.

French Alps ▼

A popular destination for skiers, snowboarders, and mountaineers, the French Alps have plenty to offer less adventurous visitors—picturesque villages, luxurious resorts, and breathtaking scenery.

Kalalau Valley (Hawaii) ▶

This valley is accessible only by boat (when the seas are tranquil in summer) or by way of the 18-kilometer Kalalau Trail. The remote valley is known for its steep cliffs and diverse selection of plant and animal life. It's a great place to get away from it all.

Antigua, Guatemala ▶

This colorful city is famous for its old Spanish architecture and traditional crafts. Tourists come to Antigua for its charm and convenience—it's the perfect spot for starting your exploration of the rest of the country after you finish sightseeing in the city.

C   Think about a popular vacation spot that you know well. Tell a partner about this vacation spot using the vocabulary from this page. Be sure to explain what the destination is known for and what one can do there.

Grand Lake is a popular vacation destination. I like it because it's accessible . . .

Grammar

Uses of Infinitives and Gerunds

1. purpose infinitive	Last summer I went overseas **to study** English.
2. *it + be* + adjective + infinitive	It was great **to experience** life in a small town.
3. *too* + adjective + infinitive	At first, it was too hard **to communicate** in English.
4. gerunds as subjects	**Learning** the language was essential.
5. adjective + preposition + gerund	The small town is famous for **skiing** in the winter and **hiking** in the summer.
6. verb + preposition + gerund	I look forward to **going back** next year!

verb + preposition + gerund: dream of ~, look forward to ~, plan on ~, talk about ~, think about ~

adjective + preposition + gerund: afraid of ~, excited about ~, known / famous for ~, interested in ~

A Read about these two events happening around the world. Complete the sentences with the gerund or infinitive form of the verb in parentheses.

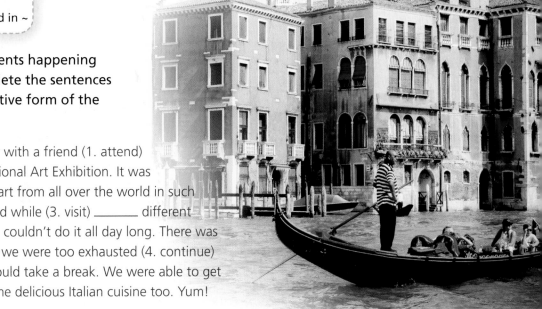

Last summer, I went to Italy with a friend (1. attend) _____ the Venice International Art Exhibition. It was wonderful (2. see) _____ art from all over the world in such a beautiful atmosphere. And while (3. visit) _____ different exhibits is entertaining, you couldn't do it all day long. There was a lot to see! On days when we were too exhausted (4. continue) _____, my friend and I would take a break. We were able to get away (5. enjoy) _____ some delicious Italian cuisine too. Yum!

I've been interested in samba (6. dance) _____ for a long time, so (7. visit) _____ Rio de Janeiro on National Samba Day sounds like a lot of fun. First you dance in the central train station. If you're planning on (8. dance) _____ some more, get on a "party train." You may think the train is too crowded (9. enjoy) _____ yourself, but there's live music and everyone has a great time! The train's destination is the suburban neighborhood of Oswaldo Cruz. People go there (10. hear) _____ free concerts.

B Now write about a place you visited recently. Complete these sentences first and use them as the basis for a more complete description. Then tell a partner about your trip.

I went to __Place__ to . . .

It was too __Adjective__ to . . . while we were there.

It's known for . . .

It was great to . . .

. . . was the best part of our trip.

I plan on . . .

Listening

A How much do you know about China's capital city Beijing?
Choose your answers.

1. What does the name *Beijing* mean?
   a. Eternal City   b. Northern Capital   c. City of Knowledge

2. The Forbidden City (pictured) is a popular tourist destination.
   What was it originally?
   a. a market place   b. a large cemetery   c. a palace

3. What is the nickname of the stadium built for the 2008
   Summer Olympic Games?
   a. Power Palace   b. Golden Egg   c. Bird's Nest

B Listen to a walking tour of Beijing. There are eight stops on the tour.
On the map, write each location next to (a) in each box.

TIP When you have to write information quickly, such as when you take notes, it helps to use abbreviations or symbols. For example: *bookstore* bkst 📖

Make your own abbreviations or symbols for these places: *bridge, building, hotel, library, museum, plaza*. What other places might be part of a walking tour?

C Listen again and take notes on any interesting facts or things you can do in each place.
Write your notes next to (b) in each box.

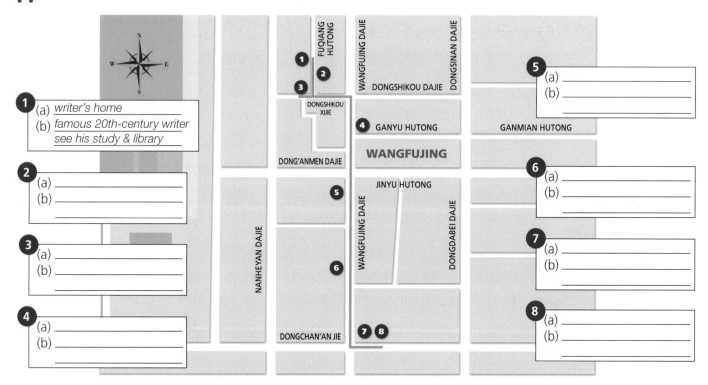

①
(a) *writer's home*
(b) *famous 20th-century writer see his study & library*

D Using your notes, take turns telling a partner about each place on the walking tour. Say what each place is and give at least one fact about it. Which place would you be most interested to visit?

Connections

A You are going to make your own walking tour. Follow the steps below.

1. Which places in your city or area would be interesting for tourists to visit? List as many neighborhoods, streets, or areas as you can.

 2. Work with a partner. Compare your ideas in step 1. Together, choose <u>one</u> neighborhood or area to feature in your walking tour.

3. What things can people do and see in this area? With your partner, think of eight ideas and create a chart using the categories below.

   A walking tour of:

   Cultural Sites   Food   Shopping   Activities

4. Choose six places from step 3. On a separate piece of paper, you should each draw a map of the area. Number each place 1–6, but do not write each place's name. Make sure you each have your own copy of the map.

5. On another piece of paper, create your walking tour. Make notes for yourselves about the places on the tour, including one interesting fact about each location. Work together, but make sure you each have your own copy of the tour.

> **TIP** Using adjectives can make each place on your tour sound more interesting. Think of adjectives you can use to describe each place.

B Now work with a new partner. Role-play the walking tour. Then switch roles and repeat.

Tour Guide: Give your map to your partner. Then start your walking tour.

Tourist: Listen to your partner's walking tour. Label each destination (1–6) on the map. Note any interesting facts that your partner tells you about each place.

I recommend visiting the Nine Streets neighborhood in Amsterdam. Shopping is an adventure here: you can find everything from luxurious shops to simple bakeries. Our first stop is a little shop that is famous for its delicious tea. It's a small place, always busy, but full of charm and never too crowded to visit. Step inside to learn all about tea-making in Holland. You might be interested to know that . . .

Ask

Answer   What was most interesting about your partner's walking tour? What is something new you learned about the area?

Reading

A You are going to read an interview with singer Jason Mraz. First, read the interview questions below. With a partner, scan each of Mraz's responses on p. 19. Then write the letter of the question in the box beside each response. (One of the questions is extra.)

A What has really surprised you in your travels?

B Are there places you haven't been to yet that you want to visit?

C How do your travel experiences influence your music?

D Tell us about your book of Polaroid® travel photography.

E Is there more to say about your writing?

F What style of traveler are you?

Jason Mraz, pop singer-songwriter

B Read the interview. Then read the statements below. Which ones apply to Jason Mraz?

1. ☐ I plan everything before I go anywhere.
2. ☐ I like to wander (walk around without a specific purpose).
3. ☐ I think people everywhere are more alike than they are different.
4. ☐ I like to write down my experiences.
5. ☐ I have a new camera so I take as many photos as possible.
6. ☐ You need to go far away to have interesting experiences.

C Why is each place significant for Jason? With a partner, discuss at least one reason for each location.

Paris   New York   San Diego   Japan   Antarctica

D Find a word or expression . . .

1. in paragraph 1 that means *well-known buildings or sites.* _____
2. in paragraph 1 that means *to finally arrive somewhere after a while.* _____
3. in paragraph 1 that means *to hurry.* _____
4. in paragraph 1 that means *done in a sudden or unplanned way.* _____
5. in paragraph 2 that means *shy and nervous.* _____
6. in paragraph 2 that means *a person who doesn't belong to a group.* _____
7. in paragraph 3 that means *choose very carefully; not easy to please.* _____
8. in paragraph 4 that means *a way of seeing or thinking about something.* _____
9. in paragraph 5 that means *being alone.* _____

Ask

Answer Look back at the statements in Exercise **B**. Which ones are true for you? What are some of your favorite travel memories?

Traveling Troubadour[1]

by Keith Bellows

1 A spontaneous one, with little preparation. I pack light. I don't feel a need to rush through all the major landmarks. Like, if I go to Paris, I might just take a walk, with no map or tourist site in mind, and end up in a neighborhood coffee shop. I guess I'm a traveler who likes to think he's not traveling. That's how I ended up in San Diego. I traveled there and found this great coffee shop that I love to make music in and I ended up staying. I've lived there for twelve years now.

10 I'm constantly surprised that no matter where I go, people are similar, just trying to make it.[2] We're all quiet and shy in an elevator with other people. Before I ever traveled to Japan I thought maybe it would be like another planet. But when I got there I realized, oh, these are just humans over here doing the same human thing, perhaps with different resources. It made me feel less timid about going places and more able to just walk through a village in, say, Ghana—or anywhere else in the world—looking like an obvious outsider. I'm comfortable with that.

20 I often keep a travel journal. I'll just sit on the steps somewhere and write. A journal that I bought is the best souvenir. It allows me to relive my memories of places around the world. At one point I started to travel with a Polaroid[3] 600 instant camera. I could just snap a picture[4] and put it right in with my journal entry. With a Polaroid, you never know what you'll get. Because Polaroid film is so rare and slightly expensive, I became very particular about what I shot. With a digital camera I might take a hundred pictures in a matter of minutes,

30 but with a Polaroid, I wait to find a scene I really want to shoot. I look for scenes with depth, like a long line of lampposts. I love looking up in the trees and at buildings. When you're comfortable with a place, you forget to look up. New Yorkers never look up. Only the tourists do. Sometimes on my blog I write from a traveler's perspective. There are people who never leave their home state that rely on travel writing to help them experience more of the world. Knowing that, I also encourage people to explore places

40 near their own communities. I grew up in Mechanicsville, Virginia, for example, which is rich with history. Every time I go home, I do something I missed growing up, such as visiting a historic battlefield.[5]

> I guess I'm a traveler who likes to think he's not traveling.

50 I've always wanted to take a cruise to Antarctica to see that continent. That would be just a brilliant trip for nature, solitude, and for writing in the journal. To really see the world, you should visit all seven continents, and that is the only one I have not been to.

[1] **troubadour** a traveling musician
[2] **make it** to be successful (in life) or survive something difficult
[3] **Polaroid** a type of camera (and film) that develops photos instantly
[4] **snap a picture** take a photo
[5] **battlefield** a place where a fight between armies has occurred

Speaking

A Read the note in the box about a bucket list. Then create your own list on a separate sheet of paper using these categories. Write at least one goal for each category.

Travel   Hobbies and Interests   Education and Career   Personal Life

I want to learn to sing. . . and I really want to visit Egypt and see the pyramids.

B Work with a partner to get advice on your bucket list. Follow the steps below. Then switch roles and repeat the activity.

Speaking Strategy	**Making Suggestions / Giving Advice**

Making Suggestions / Giving Advice
One/Another thing you could do is (*infinitive*) . . .
What/How about (*gerund*) . . . ?
Have you thought about (*gerund*) . . . ?
You talked about (*gerund*) . . . ?

Accepting Advice
Thanks. That's a good idea.
OK, I'll give it a try/shot.
That makes sense.

Questioning Advice
I thought about doing that, but . . .
One problem with that is . . .

Refusing Advice
I'm not sure that would work for me.

Student 1: Tell your partner a little about your goals. Explain how you plan to accomplish each one.

Student 2: Listen to your partner's goals and ask questions about each one. Give your partner advice. Use the expressions in the box to help you.

Student 1: Take notes on the advice your partner gives you. You can accept or question the advice.

C Repeat Exercise **B** with two new partners.

D Share your findings with the class or in a small group. Answer the questions.

1. What was the best advice you got? Why was it good advice?

2. Which of your classmates' goals did you think was the most interesting?

Video

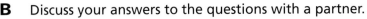

A You are going to watch a video about a street in Barcelona called Las Ramblas. First, listen to the audio (without watching) and think about these questions:

1. What do you think the street looks like? Describe it in as much detail as you can.
2. How do the speakers feel about Las Ramblas?

B Discuss your answers to the questions with a partner. Then watch the video and check your answers.

C What do the four speakers say about Barcelona and Las Ramblas? Watch the video again and match each speaker with a statement (a–f). For some speakers, more than one answer is possible.

a. In some ways, performing outside is better than in the theater.
b. There's diverse theater and music from all over the world here.
c. There's something happening at any time of day.
d. My life improved when I moved here from my country.
e. If you want to have fun, this is the best street . . . maybe in the whole world.
f. The action is out on the streets.

1. _____

2. _____

3. _____

4. _____

D What did each speaker say that made you choose your answers in Exercise **C**? Watch the video again and list the key words and phrases you hear from each speaker on a separate sheet of paper. Then compare answers with a partner.

Ask

Answer Would you like to visit Las Ramblas? Why or why not?

Writing

A Descriptive Paragraph

A Read the blog post. Then complete the steps that follow.

Abram Recommends: Las Ramblas

La Boqueria

Las Ramblas is an interesting area in Barcelona that attracts thousands of visitors every day. A number of things make Las Ramblas a favorite of both tourists and locals. The wide streets, for example, are lined with trees and picturesque buildings that are hundreds of years old. In many places, the ground is decorated with colorful tiles and mosaics.[1] Las Ramblas is also known for its lively and festive atmosphere. Diverse groups of performers from all over the world fill the streets. Day and night, the area is alive with people singing and dancing and artists selling their goods. And finally, near Las Ramblas is one of Barcelona's

[1] tiles and mosaics decorative ceramics

[2] seedy dirty, unsafe

largest produce markets: *La Boqueria*. It's the perfect place to pick up a snack.

Las Ramblas has something for everyone, but the streets can be crowded with tourists, particularly in the summer. Parts of Las Ramblas can also be a bit seedy[2] at night. Although it's best to avoid this area after dark, overall Las Ramblas is a safe and entertaining area of the city. I highly recommend it!

1. Complete the statements below with information from the reading.

   Things in Las Ramblas you can . . .

see	*lots of people, picturesque buildings*	taste	_____
hear	_____	touch	_____

2. Which adjectives does the writer use to describe Las Ramblas? Circle them in the paragraph. Which ones are positive? Which have a negative meaning? Compare your answers with a partner.

B Read the information in the Writing Strategy. Then complete the steps that follow.

1. Think of an interesting place in a city or town you know well (a street, restaurant, beach, or other location).

2. Write statements like those in Exercise **A** with information about your place. Also list relevant adjectives.

3. Use your notes to write a blog entry of your place on a separate piece of paper.

> **Writing Strategy**
>
> **Create a Mental Image** When you describe something, it's important to *show* and not just *tell* your reader information. For example, don't just say a place is beautiful or interesting; explain what makes it that way. You can help your reader visualize something by doing the following:
>
> 1. Use adjectives and descriptive phrases. OK: *There are many trees and old buildings in Las Ramblas.* Better: *The **wide** streets are **lined with trees** and **picturesque** buildings that are **hundreds of years old.***
>
> 2. Describe something in more detail with an extra sentence or two. *Las Ramblas is also known for its **lively** and **festive** atmosphere. **Diverse** groups of performers from all over the world fill the streets.*

C Exchange papers with another student. Does your partner's writing follow the Writing Strategy?

Expanding Your Fluency

A What kind of traveler are you? Mark the activities in 1–7 that apply to you. Then answer question 8.

When I'm on vacation, I want to . . .

1. ☐ get away from the city and relax in a tranquil spot.
2. ☐ sleep late and read.
3. ☐ spend some time at a luxurious spa.
4. ☐ go sightseeing every day.
5. ☐ study or learn something.
6. ☐ do a lot of shopping.
7. ☐ try the local cuisine.
8. What are two activities you like to do on vacation?

_____

> **Some Popular Vacation Activities**
>
> | | |
> |---|---|
> | surfing | playing golf |
> | waterskiing | mountain biking |
> | swimming | paragliding |
> | sunbathing | skiing |
> | hiking | snowboarding |

B Work with a partner.

Tourist: You are on vacation in an exotic city. You need help setting your itinerary for the next two days. Ask the concierge* of your hotel for advice on what to see and do in the area. Use your information from Activity **A** to get you started. Respond to the concierge's advice by accepting, questioning, or refusing.

Hotel Concierge: You are a concierge. One of your guests needs help planning an itinerary for the next two days. Ask about his or her interests. Suggest places to visit and things to do in the area. Describe in detail each place you mention.

C Change roles and repeat Activity **B**.

> Good afternoon. May I help you?

> Yes. I'm visiting for a couple of days and I'm looking for things to see and do . . .

Check What You Know

Rank how well you can perform these outcomes on a scale of 1–5 (5 being the best).

_____ use descriptive language effectively

_____ use gerund and infinitive structures to describe experiences

_____ make travel recommendations

_____ give, accept, and question advice

---

*concierge a hotel employee who helps guests arrange things (sightseeing trips, theater tickets, etc.)

3 The Great Energy Challenge

1 Do you know what these energy sources are? Use your dictionary to look up any unfamiliar words. Of the four, which one produces the most energy worldwide today? Which ones produce safe, clean energy?

   a. solar panels
   b. a nuclear reactor
   c. a wind turbine
   d. an oil rig

2 Read the unit title. What do you think an "energy challenge" is?

3 What energy challenges is the world facing now?

Unit Outcomes

In this unit, you will learn to:

- refine your use of future tenses

- identify the pros and cons of an issue

- express an opinion and give examples to support it

- persuade an audience to make a change

Vocabulary

consume to use, especially in large amounts
eliminate to remove something entirely
entire the whole of something
generate to make or produce
project to predict
rely on to depend on or use
residents the people who live in a certain place (house, neighborhood, city, etc.)

reverse to cause something to move in the opposite direction
run out to use something (up) completely
source the origin or starting place of something
supply to give an amount; provide
sustainable long-lasting or good for the environment

> **reverse** the effects (of something), ~ a decision, ~ the order, Put your car in ~.

A Read the energy statistics. Use the word bank to help you. Did any of the information surprise you? Why?

 PRONUNCIATION Notice that these two words are different. *We're launching the **PROject** next year. They **proJECT** a 10 percent increase by 2020.* For more information on heteronyms and stress shift, see page 146.

? Did you know?

- Hydro power could generate 20 percent of the energy that developed nations need.
- Wind power could supply forty times more energy than we consume now.
- One hour of sunlight can supply the world with enough energy for an entire year. Using solar energy (instead of fossil fuels) could also help reverse the effects of global warming.
- Coal, the largest source of electric power today, can be mined in a third of the world's countries.
- Experts project that natural gas will produce 26 percent of the world's energy by 2020.
- Oil powers our lives, but using oil is not sustainable and experts predict it will run out in the next century.
- Residents of France rely on nuclear power; 78 percent of the country's electricity comes from this energy source, more than any other nation in the world.

> **global warming** an increase in Earth's temperature caused by burning **fossil fuels** (oil, gas, and coal)

B Which words from the list go with *energy*? Complete the Word Partnership box.

C Discuss these questions with a partner.

1. Which energy sources does your country rely on the most?
2. Are there energy sources we should eliminate from our day-to-day lives?
3. Do you believe that oil will eventually run out completely? Why or why not?
4. What is one thing you or your community can do to consume less energy?
5. Do you think we can reverse the effects of global warming? Why or why not?

Word Partnership

Use *energy* with:
v: consume, g_____, r____ out (of), s_____ energy
n: *energy* s_____

Grammar

A Choose the best answer(s) for items 1–4. More than one option may be possible. Then explain your answers to a partner.

1. **A:** Do you want to see a movie? **B:** I can't. _____ this evening.
   a. I'm studying
   b. I'll study
   c. I'm going to study

2. Experts think the cost of solar power _____ decrease in the future.
   a. is going to
   b. will

3. a. I'll text you when I get a break.
   b. I'll text you when I'll get a break.

4. At this time tomorrow, _____ to Asia.
   a. I'll travel
   b. I'll be traveling

Review of Future Forms	
definite plans	**I'm going to take** the TOEFL next Saturday. **I'm taking** the TOEFL next Saturday.
predictions	By 2040, there **are going to be** over 8 billion people on Earth. By 2040, there **will be** over 8 billion people on Earth.
promises	**I'll call** you tonight after I get home. I **won't** forget.
ongoing future actions	Within ten years, Germany **will be using** less oil and more renewable sources.

B Complete this quiz with an appropriate future form of the verb in parentheses. Then ask and answer the questions with a partner.

1. Which country _____ (consume) the most energy in the near future?
   a. China   b. India   c. the United States

2. Which country _____ (have) the largest per person energy consumption this year?
   a. Canada   b. Russia   c. South Africa

3. What country _____ (continue) to generate the most geothermal energy?
   a. Iceland   b. Costa Rica   c. the United States

4. Which country _____ (run) 50 percent of their cars on ethanol (fuel made from corn) in the future?
   a. Mexico   b. Brazil   c. Japan

5. Global energy demand will _____ (increase) as the population _____ (increases). How much of that increase _____ (come) from the richest countries in the world?
   a. 7 percent   b. 17 percent   c. 27 percent

C Discuss these predictions with a partner. Do you agree with the statements?

In the future . . .

Fewer people will be driving gas-powered cars.
More people will rely on nuclear energy.

My country is going to be oil independent.
Your own idea: _____

Listening

A Look at these two groups of verbs in bold. What do they mean? Discuss your ideas.

1	I'm going to **reduce** my work week from forty hours to thirty. My doctor told me to **cut down** / **cut back** on desserts.
2	To be a vegetarian, you need to **eliminate** all red meat from your diet. I need to eat better, but I cannot **give up** chocolate completely. I love it too much!

B You're going to listen to the introduction to a TV program. What do you think it's about? Tell a partner. Then listen and complete the sentence in your own words.

The program Our Green Planet *will be following everyday people as they* _____.

C Listen to each person. Check (✓) the energy-saving actions that they are taking.

The Novak family

The Noguchi family

The Perez family

☐ use a bicycle instead of a car for short trips

☐ reduce air travel

☐ grow their own food

☐ unplug all electronic appliances daily

☐ change the temperature settings on the refrigerator

☐ hang clothes to dry

☐ carpool (to drive together with others)

☐ buy only locally made products

☐ use solar energy for heating water or cooking

D Look at the items in Exercise **C** that you didn't check. Why doesn't the family do these things? Listen again and take notes using the pattern below. Then explain your answers to a partner.

The _____ family doesn't _____ because . . .

Ask

Answer Mr. Noguchi counted the electronic appliances in his home. How many are in your home? In the kitchen? In the living room? In your bedroom?

Connections

A Read through the survey alone and underline any words you don't know. Then discuss
the survey as a class. Can your classmates explain the unfamiliar words to you?

ARE YOU READY TO GO ON AN ENERGY DIET?

1. _____ Eliminate at least three chemical housecleaning products.
2. _____ Buy only locally made or grown products.
3. _____ Resist the urge to buy an item that you don't use often.
4. _____ Eat a vegetarian diet one day a week.
5. _____ Grow your own food.
6. _____ Give up at least one processed food that you normally eat.
7. _____ Use public transportation at least three times a week.
8. _____ Unplug phone chargers when they are not in use.
9. _____ Give up bottled water for tap water.
10. _____ Turn off the tap when you're brushing your teeth.
11. _____ Recycle all glass, aluminum, plastic, and paper.
12. _____ Eliminate the use of plastic and paper bags
when shopping.

Chicago waterfront

B Working alone, take the survey above. Write
the letter of a statement below (*a, b, c, d*)
next to each item in the energy diet survey.

a. I do this already.
b. I'll try to do this in the next month.

c. I'm going to do this someday in the future.
d. I can't do this. It seems impossible.

C Compare your answers with a partner. How similar or different are you?

D Look at your **b** and **c** answers in the energy diet survey. Complete these sentences and talk about
your personal energy diet plan.

Starting this weekend, one change I'll make is _____ .

After I make my first change, I'll _____ .

When I get discouraged about sticking to my energy diet, I'm going to _____

_____ .

By this time next year, I think I'll be _____ .

Reading

A Take the quiz and compare ideas with a partner.
Then scan the reading to check your answers.

SOLAR ENERGY Quiz

1. The sun generates more energy than humans can use.   **T**   **F**

2. Worldwide, most electricity is produced using solar energy.   **T**   **F**

3. Solar energy generates a lot of pollution.   **T**   **F**

4. Solar energy can only be used in places that get a lot of sunlight all year.   **T**   **F**

B Why aren't we using solar power more? List some of your ideas. Then read the passage to check your answers.

C Read the passage again. On a separate piece of paper, list at least two advantages and two disadvantages of each method of gathering solar energy (steam generation and PV panels).

> **Reading Strategy**
>
> **Identifying key details** The article compares two ways of gathering solar energy. As you read, watch for keywords like *advantage, disadvantage, drawback, however, (al)though,* and *on the other hand* to help you identify key details.

D Use your answers from Exercise **C** to act out this role-play.

1. **Student A:** Imagine that you work for a solar energy company. You need to persuade the mayor of your city to invest more money in solar power. Give two or three reasons why this is a good idea.

   Student B: Listen to your partner's argument and ask at least two questions about the disadvantages. Did your partner convince you to invest more money?

2. Switch roles and practice again.

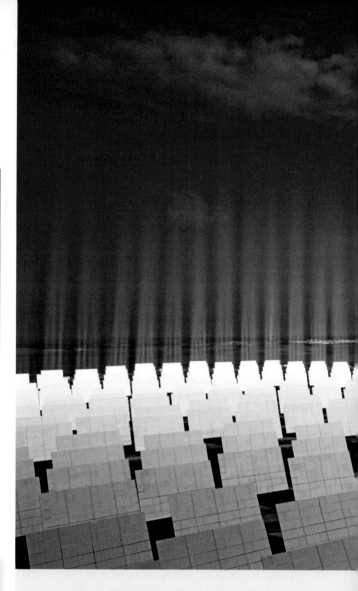

1   Our sun is the most powerful source of energy on Earth. Worldwide, humans use about 16 terawatts[1] of energy a year. The sun produces 120,000 terawatts annually—much more than we consume. Today, though, solar power is used very little; it generates less than one-tenth of 1 percent (0.1%) of the world's electricity each year.

Why don't we use solar power more? To answer this question, it's important to understand
10   the two main ways we gather energy from the sun. The first way is to place flat, computer-guided mirrors in a field. The mirrors focus sunlight onto a receiver on a tower and this produces steam. The steam is then used to produce electricity. The second way of gathering energy from the sun is to use PV (photovoltaic) panels. The panels collect sunlight and convert[2] it into electricity. Most people have seen PV panels on buildings; small ones are also on some handheld calculators.

20   Both ways of gathering solar energy have their advantages. Unlike oil or coal, solar power

The SUN

Sunlight provides us with more energy than we need . . .
so why aren't we using solar power more?

generates "clean" energy that produces very little pollution. However, the steam-generation method[3] is more efficient than the PV panel method because it converts more sunlight into electricity. The steam generation method requires a lot of open space, though (for example, a big field). Long cables are also needed to transmit[4] the power from an open space to the city, which can be expensive. PV panels, on the other hand, can easily be placed on rooftops where the power is needed. There is no extra cost to transmit the energy in this way.

Both methods have a similar disadvantage: they are unable to produce enough energy when it's cloudy or dark. Engineers are working on this problem. For now, though, people who use PV panels as their main source of energy must rely on batteries at night or when the weather is bad.

One of solar energy's biggest drawbacks is cost. PV panels are still very expensive to buy. In some places, though, people are earning their money

back. Wolfgang Schnürer lives in Freiburg, Germany. He powers his home using solar energy. In the winter, the panels on the roof of Schnürer's apartment do not produce enough energy. But on a sunny day in May, the panels can generate *more* energy than he and his family consume. When this happens, Schnürer can sell the extra power back to the energy company in his city. In 2008, he made 2,500 euros ($3,700) from the extra power his solar panels generated.

Despite the challenges, solar energy use is increasing worldwide. In Germany, Japan, and the United States, governments are trying to make solar power more affordable for everyone. And as people find that they can save money—and even make money—using solar power, the number of countries using this energy source will surely grow.

[1] **terawatt** a measurement of electrical power
[2] **convert** change
[3] **method** a way of doing something
[4] **transmit** send from one place to another place

Video

A In this video, you are going to meet Lauren, a Greenpeace activist. Read about Greenpeace below. Have you ever heard of it?

Greenpeace is the largest environmental organization in the world. It works to protect our oceans and forests and stop global warming. Greenpeace activists (people who work to achieve social or political change) sometimes take the initiative in effecting changes instead of working with political leaders, even to the extent of breaking the law.

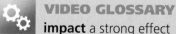
B Watch the video once through with the *sound off*. What energy issue is the video about? Then watch the video with the *sound on* and check your ideas.

C Watch and answer these questions by completing each blank with the correct word.

What is the problem? (1) _____ (2) _____ energy is something the United States has been (3) _____ (4) _____ for way too long.

What does Lauren think is a basic human right? Having (5) _____ (6) _____

What has the plant been doing? (7) _____ a significant amount of (8) _____ to the community

What does the community want to do? They want to (9) _____ the coal plant (10) _____ (11) _____ .

D Watch again and answer these questions. If an answer isn't given, write "NM" ("not mentioned").

1. What is Lauren deeply concerned about?
2. How does Lauren feel about the plant?
3. What does Lauren say the plant is a roadblock to?
4. According to Lauren, what can people do to stop the plant?

E Discuss these questions with a partner.

1. Do you think it's sometimes all right to get people to make changes without involving the proper authorities?
2. Lauren says, "Sometimes we need to be leaders ourselves." Do you agree with this statement?
3. Lauren is protesting at the plant in Bridgeport, Connecticut. What other things could people in that community do to shut down the plant?

Writing
A Persuasive Paragraph

A Read the paragraph. Then answer the questions with a partner.

Change a Bulb, Save the Planet

Everyone wants to save energy and protect the environment. Now you can do both by using CFL bulbs instead of regular bulbs in your home, classroom, or office. How will this help? **For one thing**, according to National Geographic's *Lightbulb Buying Guide*, CFL bulbs use almost 75% less energy than regular bulbs. When we use less energy to light a room, we generate less CO_2. This helps the environment. **In addition**, because CFL bulbs use less energy, you'll save a lot of money on your electric bill over time. So remember: a regular bulb will light your home. However, a CFL bulb will help you save energy, spend less on electricity, and improve the environment. You can make a difference!

TIP The writer uses specific facts to support his point. He cites his source by using the words *according to*.

1. What is the main goal of this paragraph?

    a. to compare two similar things
    b. to explain why you should do something
    c. to describe the pros and cons of something

2. What two benefits are discussed in the paragraph? Which words introduce these ideas?

B Read the Writing Strategy. What do you notice about the words that follow *instead of*, *rather than*, and *by*?

C You want to encourage people to change something they are doing now. Use the structures in the Writing Strategy and the information below. Write each sentence in two ways.

> **Writing Strategy**
>
> **Being persuasive** To encourage people to do one thing instead of another, you can use structures like these:
>
> 1. **Instead of / Rather than** <u>using</u> regular light bulbs, use CFL bulbs. You'll save energy.
> 2. **By** <u>using</u> CFL bulbs **instead of / rather than** (<u>using</u>) regular bulbs, you'll save energy.

You waste energy when you . . .

1. drive everywhere.
2. throw away paper and plastic.
3. drink bottled water.
4. always keep all electronics plugged in.
5. Your idea: _____

You save energy when you . . .

ride a bike.
recycle paper and plastic.
drink filtered water.
unplug electronics when you're not using them.
Your idea: _____

Instead of driving, ride a bike sometimes. / By riding a bike sometimes instead of driving, you'll save energy.

D Choose a sentence from Exercise **C** (1–5). On a separate piece of paper, write a paragraph that explains the change and gives two reasons why people should do it.

Everyone wants to save energy and protect the environment. Now you can do both . . .

E Exchange papers with another student. Read your partner's writing and answer questions 1–3 in the Writing Checklist.

Writing Checklist

Does the paragraph . . .

1. clearly state what change people should make?
2. give two reasons to make the change, using *for one thing* and *in addition*?
3. convince readers to change their behavior?

Speaking

A Work with a partner. You are going to create a public service announcement* about saving energy. Choose an idea from Exercise **C** on page 33 or think of your own. Then do the following:

Design a public service announcement that is 45–60 seconds long. It should . . .

• explain what change people should make.
• give 2–3 reasons why people should make the change.
• be interesting and make your viewers want to make the change.

For ideas, reread the paragraph and information in the Writing Strategy box on page 33 again.

B Do your presentations.

Presenters: Present your public service announcement to the class.

Viewers: Take notes on each pair's public service announcement. Answer these questions briefly:

1. What change do they want you to make?
2. What reasons did they give for making the change?
3. Did they convince you to make a change? Why or why not?

C Compare your notes in Exercise **B** with a partner. In your opinion, which public service announcement was the best? Why?

*A public service announcement is an ad that tells people about an important issue.

Expanding Your Fluency

A We can add the suffixes *-ion / -tion / -sion* to some verbs to form nouns. Complete the chart with the noun or verb form of each word. Use your dictionary to help you. Then say the words with a partner.

Verb	Noun
1. consume	
2.	conversion
3. eliminate	
4. generate	
5.	pollution

Verb	Noun
6. prevent	
7.	production
8.	projection
9. reduce	
10.	transmission

B Use the correct words from the chart to complete the sentences. Check answers with a partner.

1. How is the air quality in your city? Is there a lot of _____ or is the air clean?
2. Should we completely _____ cars in cities and encourage people to walk and bike only?
3. What things can you do to cut down on energy _____ and _____ your electric bill each month so that you pay less?
4. Which sources _____ the most energy today? Are there any energy sources we should stop using? Why?

C Think about your answers to the questions in Exercise **B**. Then do the following with a partner.

1. Take turns. Choose one of the questions.
2. Answer the question by talking for one minute without stopping, and you get a point.
3. Repeat steps 1 and 2 for a total of ten minutes. Continue until there are no more questions or the ten minutes are up.
4. The winner is the person with the most points at the end.

Check What You Know

Rank how well you can perform these outcomes on a scale of 1–5 (5 being the best).

_____ refine your use of future tenses

_____ identify the pros and cons of an issue

_____ express an opinion and give examples to support it

_____ persuade an audience to make a change

4 The World's a Stage

1 Where do you think this photo was taken? What type of music do you think is being played?

2 Do you think this performer is famous? What's more important, being famous no matter what or staying true to your roots?

3 Who are some of your favorite musicians and actors? Do you ever go to see live performances?

Unit Outcomes

In this unit, you will learn to:

- use infinitives to complement certain types of verbs

- state the pros and cons of making a decision

- use time expressions to order life events

- paraphrase information from other sources

Vocabulary

A Your friend is a musician who wants to become famous. What would you tell him or her to do? Think of two or three ideas with a partner and then share them with the class.

audience a group of people watching a performance
commercial related to the buying and selling of goods and services
convince to persuade someone (to do something)
emerge to come out and be recognized or noticed
hard-core very committed (to something)

inspired (by) encouraged (by) or motivated (by)
launch to start
mainstream most typical or conventional
make an appearance to come out in public
performance singing, dancing, or acting for an audience

> **commercial** ~ *success*, ~ *development*, ~ *use*

> Which of the following *-ance* words are formed from verbs? From adjectives? *assistance, brilliance, disturbance, entrance, importance*

B Read this profile of Esmee Denters and answer the questions below with a partner.

This is the story of a 17-year-old Dutch teenager with a webcam and a dream. Esmee Denters loved to sing and her friends loved her voice. They convinced her to launch her own YouTube channel. Inspired by her friends' support, Esmee started recording videos. And they were soon a hit. Within nine months, her videos had 21 million views, and, just like any celebrity, she had hard-core fans. Esmee had definitely arrived on the scene.

Her big commercial break came when singer Justin Timberlake contacted her. They wrote several songs together. Esmee put out an album and even made an appearance on *The Oprah Winfrey Show*. The webcam singer was soon giving performances for audiences of 70,000 people. Unbelievably, with almost no attention from the mainstream media, the pancake waitress from the suburbs had emerged as a star!

1. Who convinced her to launch a YouTube channel?
2. When did her big commercial break happen?
3. Where did she make an appearance?
4. What is her relationship to the mainstream media?

C Think of a singer that you like, but don't tell your partner his or her name. Your partner will ask you questions about your choice to guess your singer.

> She sang the official song for the 2010 World Cup.

> What's one of her most famous songs?

Grammar

A Complete these sentences with *to, for,* or — (nothing).

1. They made me _____ practice every day.
2. We'll arrange _____ you _____ pick up the tickets.
3. They advised us _____ take the offer.

Infinitive Complements

Infinitive complements that follow the pattern **verb + object + infinitive** fall into some common verb groups including ❶ *persuade* verbs (*advise, cause, convince*), ❷ *want* verbs (*expect, need*), ❸ *believe* verbs (*consider, recognize*), and ❹ *plan* verbs (*arrange*). Group ❺ verbs are *have, let,* and *make.*

❶ Verb + object + infinitive	She **advised** me **to take** the job.
❷ Verb + (object) + infinitive	She **expects** me **to apply**. I **need to find** a job.
❸ Verb + object + infinitive of *be*	We **consider** him **to be** the best singer.
❹ Verb + *for* + object + infinitive	They **arranged for** me **to have** an interview.
❺ Verb + object + base form	His music **makes** me **feel** happy.

Group ❶: the object is required.   Group ❷: the object is optional.
Group ❸: follows the pattern **verb + object + infinitive**, and the infinitive is usually *to be*.
Group ❹: follows the pattern **verb + *for* + object + infinitive**.
Group ❺: follows the same basic pattern, but requires the base form of the verb rather than the full infinitive.

B Read this story about Bree. The structure **verb + (object) + infinitive** appears nine times. Seven of them contain errors. Find and correct the errors. Compare your answers with a partner.

Just Acting or the Real Thing? This is the story of Bree, who became an Internet celebrity. To her hard-core fans, she was a young girl who posted videos from her bedroom about her life as a teenager. Her fans (1) <u>wanted to hear</u> from her frequently. They (2) <u>expected her post</u> videos four or five times a week. They posted notes to her and (3) <u>advised to her to share</u> more about her life.

The reality, however, was quite different: a man named Ramesh Flinders produced Bree's videos. He (4) <u>arranged to an actress to play</u> the part of 15-year-old Bree. Jessica Rose, a 19-year-old actress, had a paid job pretending to be Bree. The fans didn't know a thing. They simply (5) <u>considered Bree to have</u> a normal teenage girl.

After four months, a newspaper reporter discovered the secret. The producers (6) <u>had Jessica to tell</u> the truth in one of her videos. They (7) <u>planned Bree's story to continue</u>, but it was too late. The news of the fake story (8) <u>caused viewers to stop</u> watching.

Why did Mr. Flinders (9) <u>let everyone to believe</u> that Bree was a real person? And why did Jessica do it? What do you think?

C What do you think of Bree's story? Use the verbs in the chart to discuss her story with a partner.

> I don't think anyone expected Bree to be an actress.

> I don't think it was OK to let the audience believe her story. That's dishonest.

Listening

A What do you know about salsa? Do you like it? Discuss in pairs.

Salsa Music: Quick Facts

- a merging of musical styles from Cuba, Puerto Rico, Mexico, and South America
- the name "salsa" was created in New York City in the 1960s
- Colombian salsa, Cuban salsa, and other styles have emerged over the years

audition a short performance given by a person to demonstrate suitability for a show
promote to encourage the popularity or sale of something
realize to understand something, sometimes suddenly

TIP As you listen, notice how the word *into* is used to express interest in casual speech. *I **was into** skateboarding.* (I was interested in skateboarding and enjoyed doing it.) *I finally **got into** salsa music.* (I became interested in and started enjoying salsa music.)

B Listen and choose the correct answer(s).

1. What was Carlos interested in at first?
   a. rock music   **b.** salsa music   **c.** skateboarding

2. Who has Carlos played music with?
   a. Ben   **b.** his brother   **c.** his friends

3. Why does he like salsa?
   a. It's energetic.   **b.** It's easy to dance to.   **c.** It makes him happy.

4. How is his band different?
   a. They play covers.   **b.** They write their own music.   **c.** They play an older kind of salsa.

5. Who inspires Carlos?
   a. his brother   **b.** his record company   **c.** his fans

C Listen again and put these events in order.

_____ **a.** Carlos formed a band.
__1__ **b.** Ben quit the school band.
_____ **c.** Carlos studied music.
_____ **d.** Carlos made an album.
_____ **e.** Carlos played in small bars.
_____ **f.** Carlos sang in his friend's band.

D Use the information in Exercises **B** and **C** to summarize Carlos's story in pairs.

Ask
Answer   What kind of music are you into? What's popular now?

Connections

A Read this information about fundraising. Look up any words you don't know in your dictionary.

Fundraising is a way for schools and other organizations to raise money for a particular purpose, for example, a **charity**. A common way to fund-raise is to hold a **benefit** (a sporting event / a performance / a movie screening) and sell tickets for the event. The money earned from the ticket sales is given to the school or organization.

B You are planning a benefit to raise money for your school. You need to organize an event. With a partner, answer the questions on a separate piece of paper.

Event type What type of benefit event will you have?

Entertainment You need a famous person or group to come to your event. Who will you invite? What do you want him / her / them to do at your event?

Venue Where will you have the event? Who will arrange for the space?

Schedule When will you hold the event?

Publicity How will you promote the event?

Event goals How many people do you expect to attend? How much money do you expect to earn from this event?

C Share your ideas with the class. Take notes on what your classmates say.

We are going to have _____Name_____ make an appearance at our benefit because . . .

We are going to let people know about the event by _____.

We will promote ticket sales by _____.

We expect _____ people to attend.

We hope to raise _____ by the end of the event.

a benefit movie screening

D Which fundraising plan is most likely to succeed? Vote to choose the best idea for a fundraiser.

a benefit dance performance

Reading

A Look at the photos and read the title of the article, the captions, and the quote. What do you think the reading is going to be about? Complete the sentence below with a partner.

This story is about _____ who lives in
_____ and wants to _____.

B Scan the article. Which of these things has Assane done? Mark your answers.

☐ written songs about his life experiences ☐ worked at the same job for all of his life

☐ experienced difficulties in his life ☐ written about pop culture

☐ lived in different places ☐ shared his creativity with others

C Read the article. As you read, look for these place names. Why does / did Assane go to each one? On a separate piece of paper, write about each place.

1. Dakar
2. Toubab Dialaw

3. the Great Rock
4. Chez Las

D With a partner, look at this sentence from the fourth paragraph. How are the underlined words similar? What is Assane trying to emphasize?

It has always existed here, because of our <u>pain</u> *and our* <u>hardships</u> *and our* <u>suffering</u>.

E How does Assane feel about these things? What does he say about them? Discuss your answers with a partner.

1. hip-hop music (first paragraph)
2. the life of a village fisherman
3. his town

4. his relatives
5. making a record
6. rap music (third paragraph)
7. money

Toubab Dialaw, Senegal

Hip-Hop
GOES HOME

The voice of a generation demanding to be heard

1 Assane N'Diaye, 19, loves hip-hop music. Before he
left his Senegalese village to work as a DJ in Dakar, he
was a fisherman, just like his father, like his father's
father before him. Tall, lean, with a muscular build and
a handsome face, Assane became a popular DJ, but the
equipment he used was borrowed, and when his friend
took it back, he returned to his village of Toubab Dialaw.
The village is located about 25 miles (40 kilometers)
south of Dakar—marked by a huge boulder, perhaps
10 40 feet (12 meters) high—facing the Atlantic Ocean.

In the shadow of this Great Rock, Assane has built
a small restaurant, Chez Las, decorated with hundreds
of seashells. It is where he lives his hip-hop dream. At
night, he and his brother and cousin sit by the Great
Rock and face the sea. They write rap songs about their
difficult lives as village fishermen, and about being poor,
watching their town get crowded with rich Dakarians
and even richer French. And they write about their
relatives who leave in the morning and never return,
20 losing their lives in the dangerous seas.

Their dream, of course, is to make a record. They
have their own demo,[1] their own logo,[2] and their own
rap group name, Salam T. D. (which stands for Toubab
Dialaw). But rap music represents a bigger dream: a
better life. "We want money to help our parents," Assane
says over dinner. "We watch our mothers boil water to
cook and have nothing to put in the pot."

He fingers[3] his food lightly. "Rap doesn't belong to
American culture," he says. "It belongs here. It has always
30 existed here, because of our pain and our hardships and
our suffering."

After a dinner of chicken and rice, Assane says
something in Wolof[4] to the others. Silently and carefully,
they take every bit of the leftover dinner—the half-eaten
bread, rice, pieces of chicken, the chicken bones—and
dump them into a plastic bag to give to the children in
the village. They silently rise from the table, walk outside,
and head out to the darkened village, holding on to that
bag as though it held money.

" Rap doesn't belong to
American culture. It
belongs here. It has
always existed here. "

[1] **demo** a brief recording illustrating the abilities of a musician
[2] **logo** a special design used by a company or group
[3] **fingers** touches
[4] **Wolof** one of many recognized regional languages of Senegal

The World's a Stage 43

Video

encounter to meet

enthusiasm a feeling of energetic interest in something

Sean-nós traditional "old style" Irish singing that combines oral history and song
Gaelic a language spoken in parts of Scotland and Ireland

Dublin

Cork

A You are going to watch a video about Iarla Ó Lionáird, a singer from Ireland. First, read these definitions. What else do you know about Ireland? Discuss with a partner.

B Look at this list of events in Iarla's life. Then, watch the video. As you watch, put the events in the order in which they happened.

_____ a. started school

_____ b. joined the Afro-Celt Sound System

_____ c. started singing traditional music for audiences worldwide

_____ d. was encouraged to sing by his teacher

_____ e. became frustrated

___1___ f. learned to sing traditional Irish music with his family

_____ g. quit singing

C Read what Iarla and the narrator said. Pay attention to the underlined words. Watch the video again and match the sentence to its meaning.

___c___ 1. It was almost as if there was—there were kind of shoes (and) they were waiting for me to put my feet into it.

_____ 2. I felt a little bit like a museum piece, really.

_____ 3. That was like the coldest breakfast you ever had to eat.

_____ 4. Frustrated, despairing, Iarla found himself on a dead-end street.

_____ 5. He quit singing entirely until fortune revealed a path.

_____ 6. I suppose it just shook me to the foundations, you know.

a. It seemed that my music was old-fashioned and no one cared about it.

b. He was stuck and he didn't know what to do next.

c. Everyone was expecting me to carry on the singing tradition.

d. The experience had a strong impact on me.

e. It was something unpleasant that I experienced.

f. Luckily, he realized what to do next.

West Cork, Ireland

Ask

Answer

What do you think is the definition of success for Iarla, making money or having an audience? What would it be for you? The enthusiasm of a few fans? Commercial success?

Writing

A Profile

A   Use the time expressions in the box to complete the profile.

as an adult	from an early age	in those days	up to that point	today

Iarla was born into a family of singers in West Cork, Ireland. (1) <u>In those days</u>, his family were known Sean-nós performers. (2) _____, Iarla was encouraged to sing. (3)_____, Iarla was living in the capital city of Dublin. The Sean-nós style was not so popular there. (4)_____, Iarla had only performed traditional music. He felt lost. He wrote a letter to Real World Records, asking for an audition. His heartfelt letter and his music convinced them to give him a contract. At Real World Records, he met the Afro-Celt Sound System and joined their band. He learned a new style of music, but never forgot his roots. (5)_____ Iarla tours the world and is loved by audiences. He inspires me because he's an excellent singer who stayed true to his roots, but he also was not afraid to try something new.

> **TIP** Time expressions like these help your reader identify key events in a person's life.

B   Follow the Writing Strategy and paraphrase each sentence below on a separate piece of paper.

> **Writing Strategy**
>
> **Paraphrasing** To paraphrase something means to express the same meaning by using different (your own) words. This is an important strategy when using information from a source (such as a book or Web site) in your own writing. Follow these steps to paraphrase:
>
> 1. Read the information and make sure you understand it.
> 2. Rewrite the main ideas using your own words.
> 3. Reread the original to make sure your version has not changed the basic meaning.
> 4. Put in quotation marks any phrases that you take directly from the original.

1. Singer Esmee Denters launched her own YouTube channel, and soon it became a big hit.

    Esmee Denters started to post her music online. Soon she had a big audience for her videos.

2. Her big break came when singer Justin Timberlake contacted her.

3. In time, with almost no attention from the mainstream media, she emerged as a star!

4. Today, she gives performances to audiences of 70,000 people or more worldwide.

C   Write a profile of a musician or other person that you like, using Exercise **A** as a model.

1. Choose a person—what qualities make him or her special or interesting? Make notes.
2. What are some important events in the person's life? Make a timeline and list time expressions you can use.
3. How has the person inspired or impacted you? Make notes for your conclusion.
4. What are the best places to find information about this person? List three sources.
5. Use your notes and timeline to write a profile. Be sure to paraphrase the information you find from your sources.

D   Exchange papers with another student. Read your partner's writing. Does it use time expressions well to describe major events in the person's life? Does it give you a clear idea of who the person is?

Speaking

A Answer these questions about Assane N'Diaye, the undiscovered musician who was featured in the reading on page 43.

1. What's his life like?
2. Who are the important people in his life?
3. What's his dream?

B Imagine that Assane has just been discovered by a talent scout who works for Global Rhythms Corporation (GRC), a recording company. They want Assane to sign a contract and leave his village in Africa. Follow these steps:

- Read the terms of the GRC contract below. Make sure you understand them.
- Discuss the terms of the contract with a partner. What do you think of it? What parts of the contract might be difficult for Assane to fulfill?
- Use the expressions in the Speaking Strategy to discuss the pros and cons of the contract.

- Assane will sign a five-year contract. GRC will arrange for Assane to live alone in an apartment in London for six months. (Assane will need to leave his family behind.)
- Assane will produce one or two albums per year. A producer will have final say in which songs get chosen for the album.
- Assane will perform and promote his music 150 days a year in cities around the world.
- Sixty percent of Assane's earnings will go to GRC. Assane will use the remaining 40% to cover his living expenses while performing on the road.
- Assane will be given a new stage name ("MC Cube") and a new style of dress.

Speaking Strategy

Giving the pros (plus sides) and cons (downsides) of something

On the one hand . . . / On the other hand . . .

A(n) (dis)advantage of this contract is . . .
One major / minor benefit of signing is . . .
One big / small drawback to signing is . . .
The best / worst part is . . .

> The best part is Assane gets to move to London!

> Yeah, but a major drawback is he has to go by himself. It sounds so lonely.

C You are going to role-play a conversation between Assane and his possible future manager at GRC.

Student A: You are Assane. You want to sign the contract, but there are some parts of it you don't like. For the cons in the contract, suggest other ideas.

Student B: You work for GRC. You want Assane to sign the contract. Listen to Assane's questions and decide what to do.

> I'm excited about living in London, but I don't want to leave my brother behind. Can he come with me for the first six months?

D Now do your role-play for another pair. When you are finished, listen to their role-play.

Expanding Your Fluency

A   Read these things you can do to start conversations with people you don't know very well. Which one of these things have you tried before? Which ones are new for you?

1. Talk about popular music, TV shows, movies, or other shared cultural experiences: *I saw the first movie, but not the sequel. How was it?*
2. Talk about recent events in the news: *The traffic was terrible today. Did you hear about the accident?*
3. Make a comment about something the person is wearing: *I love the design on your scarf. Where did you get it?*
4. Ask follow-up questions: *Are you studying music (or film) at Tokyo University? How do you like it there?*

B   Imagine that you are at a party with many famous singers, dancers, actors, and other creative people. Follow the steps below.

1. Take the role of a famous creative person whom you know something about.
2. You are going to meet five different people at a party. Stand up and move around the classroom. Find a partner, introduce yourself, and make small talk for two minutes.
3. Try to use at least one of the strategies in Exercise **A** with each person you meet.

> I'm not into comedy films, but this movie is special. I saw the first movie in the series, but not the sequel. How was it?

> The sequel was much better. I'm a hard-core fan now!

> I can't wait to see it. What exactly did you like about it?

TIP You can use these expressions to end your conversation. *(It's been) nice talking to you. Thanks. You too.*

Ask

Answer Who was the most interesting person you met at the party? Was it always easy to start a conversation? Why or why not?

Check What You Know

Rank how well you can perform these outcomes on a scale of 1–5 (5 being the best).

_____ use infinitives to complement certain types of verbs

_____ state the pros and cons of making a decision

_____ use time expressions to order life events

_____ paraphrase information from other sources

5 No Need to Panic

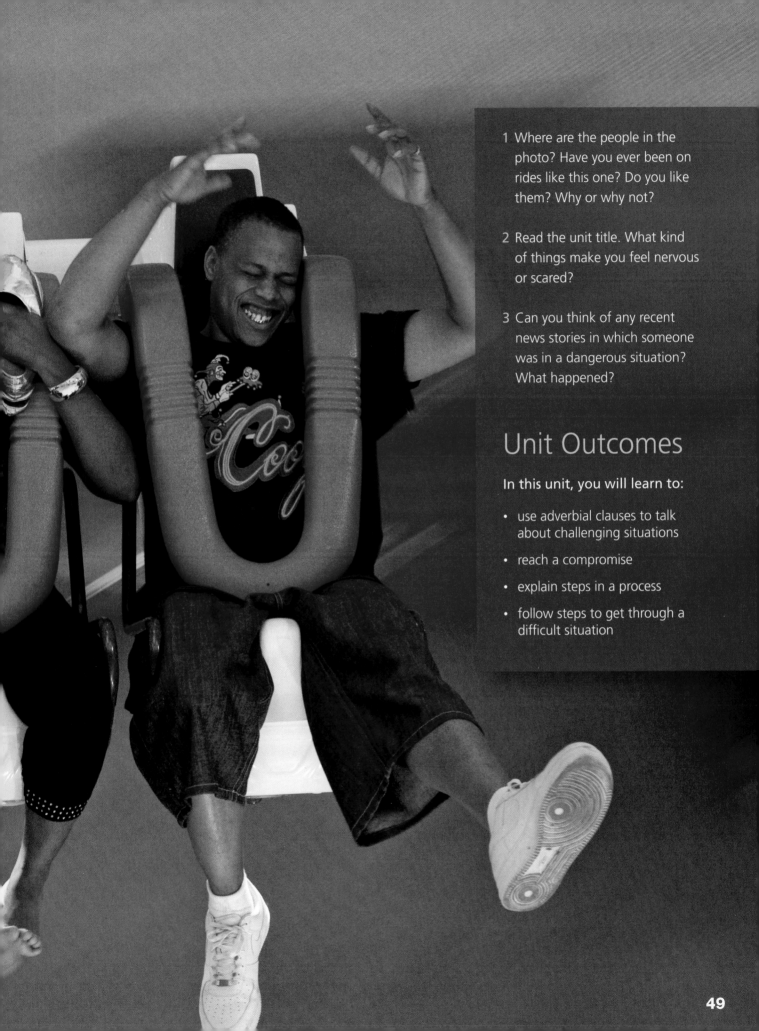

1 Where are the people in the photo? Have you ever been on rides like this one? Do you like them? Why or why not?

2 Read the unit title. What kind of things make you feel nervous or scared?

3 Can you think of any recent news stories in which someone was in a dangerous situation? What happened?

Unit Outcomes

In this unit, you will learn to:

- use adverbial clauses to talk about challenging situations

- reach a compromise

- explain steps in a process

- follow steps to get through a difficult situation

Vocabulary

collapse to fall down suddenly

encourage to give someone confidence or hope

handle to deal with a problem or situation successfully

injure to damage a part of a person's body

intense very great or extreme

ordeal a very difficult, stressful situation

panic to feel very anxious or afraid all of a sudden

rescue to save someone from a dangerous situation

trapped unable to escape from a place or situation because something is stopping you

> **n.** handle *a job* / *a problem* / *a situation*
> handle *the pressure* / *the responsibility*
> **adj.** *difficult* / *easy* / *hard to* handle

A Look at the photos and read only the titles of the two articles below. What do you think happened to these people? Use a sentence or two to describe each story to a partner.

B Read the two news articles and choose the correct option for each item.

Pilot lands plane; everyone safe

Shortly after Flight 1549 took off from New York, it lost power in both engines. The plane, flying over 3,000 feet (914 meters) in the air, was in danger of crashing. Luckily, the pilot landed safely in the Hudson River nearby. All 155 people were (1) <u>trapped / rescued</u> from the water and no one was seriously (2) <u>injured / rescued</u>. After the (3) <u>ordeal / injury</u>, survivors say that the pilot stayed calm and (4) <u>encouraged / handled</u> the situation perfectly.

Chilean miners reach the surface

After the mine they were working in (5) <u>collapsed / rescued</u>, thirty-three men were (6) <u>encouraged / trapped</u> for over ten weeks. During this time, they suffered (7) <u>intense / trapped</u> heat, a lack of food and water, and long periods of time in total darkness. One miner recalls times when he would get scared and start to (8) <u>handle / panic</u>. But whenever that happened, the others (9) <u>injured / encouraged</u> him. The men kept telling each other: "Hang in there! Help is coming!" And finally it did.

> ***Hang in there!*** – Stay positive! Don't give up! (*said to encourage someone in a difficult situation*)

C Now cover up the articles with a piece of paper. Choose <u>one</u> and explain it to your partner. Use the questions to help you.

- What happened?
- How did the people involved handle it?

Ask

Answer How do you handle scary or stressful situations—are you calm or do you start to panic? Explain with an example.

Grammar

Adverbial Clauses

Adverbial clauses explain when, why, where, or in what way something happened. Adverbial clauses begin with a *connecting word*. When the clause starts a sentence, it is followed by a comma.

Time: *after, since, whenever, as soon as, until, while, before, when*	**After the mine collapsed**, the men were trapped. The men were trapped **after the mine collapsed**.
Reason: *because, since*	**Because the mine collapsed**, the men were trapped.
Contrast: *although, (even) though*	**Even though it was hard**, they survived for weeks.
Purpose: *so (that)*	They closed the mine **so (that) an accident doesn't happen again**.
Before, after, during, since, and *until* can also be followed by a <u>noun phrase</u>.	**Before** <u>the collapse</u>, the men heard a sound. **During** <u>the collapse</u>, one man was injured.

A Tom broke his leg in a snowboarding accident. He is explaining what happened. On a separate piece of paper, combine the two sentences into a single one using the correct connecting word.

1. I went snowboarding on a difficult run. I knew it was risky. (*so that, until, even though*)

    I went snowboarding on a difficult run even though I knew it was risky. /
    Even though I knew it was risky, I went snowboarding on a difficult run.

    > **risky** dangerous
    > **risk-taker** an adventurous person, unafraid of taking chances

2. I crashed. I was coming down the mountain. (*while, whenever, since*)
3. I knew I was injured. I tried to stand up. (*so that, as soon as, until*)
4. I tried to walk. The pain was intense. (*after, though, because*)
5. My friend drove me to the hospital. I could see a doctor. (*although, so that, while*)
6. I can't snowboard. My leg is fully healed. (*so that, whenever, until*)
7. It's going to take time to get better. I was injured seriously. (*although, since, so that*)
8. I'm going to go snowboarding again. I feel better. (*as soon as, even though, while*)

B Answer these questions with a partner. Use the information in Exercise A.

1. What mistake did Tom make?
2. When did he crash?
3. When did he know he was injured?
4. Why did his friend drive him to the hospital?
5. Why is it going to take time for him to get better?
6. When can he snowboard again?

C How much of a risk-taker are you? With a partner, answer each question and explain your reasons. Use at least one connecting word from the chart in each reply.

Would you ever . . .

1. parachute (jump) out of a plane even though it's dangerous?
2. sing or play music in a public place so that you could earn some extra money?
3. cut all of your hair off or dye it so that you could have a new look?

> I'd never parachute out of a plane because I'd be too scared.

Listening

A How do the situations below make you feel? Rate each with a number: 1 (not nervous at all), 2 (somewhat nervous), or 3 (very nervous). Then explain your answers to a partner.

_____ taking an important test at school

_____ giving a presentation in front of a lot of people

_____ interviewing for a job

_____ speaking English

> Giving a presentation in front of a lot of people makes me very nervous since I don't do it often.

client someone who pays a person or company for a service; a customer

freeze (*past*: **froze**) to suddenly stop and be unable to move or think

B Listen to an interview with life coach* Greg Ravetti. Then correct these false statements.

1. Greg focuses on dangerous situations that cause anxiety.
2. One of Greg's clients recently gave a presentation at work.
3. She got so nervous that she panicked and started laughing.
4. In some situations, people panic because they're worried about their appearance.

*A **life coach** helps people set goals and improve their lives (for example, by doing better at school or work, improving their appearance, etc.).

C Greg is now going to talk about three ways to calm down in a stressful situation. Read sentences 1–3. What do you think he's going to say? Tell a partner. Then listen and complete the sentences in the first column of the chart.

Ways to calm down in a stressful situation	How doing this helps you feel calmer
1. _____ slowly for a minute.	
2. Make a simple _____. Also: Try to _____ the situation _____ you're in it.	
3. _____ the plan you created.	

D How does doing each step in Exercise **C** help you feel calmer? Listen again and take notes in the second column of the chart.

Ask

Answer — Which of Greg's recommendations do you think is the most helpful? Why?

Connections

A Listen to and read the dialog. Then answer the questions below with a partner.

Fatima: Hello?

Amina: Hey Fatima. It's Amina.

Fatima: Oh hi, Amina. What's up?

Amina: Not much. Hey, you sound upset. Are you okay?

Fatima: No, I'm freaking out. You know that project for our English class that's due tomorrow? Well I haven't started it.

Amina: What?! Why not?

Fatima: Because I thought it was due *next* week! What am I going to do? This project is 50% of our grade!

Amina: Fatima, don't panic, okay? Have you done *any* work?

Fatima: Yeah, I've got an outline.

Amina: So even though you haven't started the project, you have some ideas.

Fatima: Yeah.

Amina: Okay, just let me think for a minute . . .

1. What's Fatima's problem?
2. Is there anything positive about Fatima's situation?
3. What do you think the expression *I'm freaking out* means?

B With a partner, finish the dialog in Exercise **A** by thinking of a solution to Fatima's problem.

C Role-play your dialog for another pair. Did they like your solution?

D You are going to create a role-play that is similar to the dialog in Exercise **A**. Choose <u>one</u> of the situations below and do the following:

1. Student A: Explain to your partner what your problem is and ask for help.

   Student B: Try to calm your partner by coming up with solutions to his or her problem.

2. Practice your role-play. Be sure it includes at least three sentences with adverbial clauses.

3. Get together with another pair and role-play your entire dialog for them. Did they like your solution?

Situation 1	***The problem:*** You failed an important test because you didn't study enough. ***Why you're nervous:*** You have to tell your parents. You're not sure how they will handle the news. ***The good news:*** You're getting a good grade in the course so far.
Situation 2	***The problem:*** You borrowed your best friend's cell phone to make a call. While you were talking, you accidentally dropped it on the ground and broke it. ***Why you're nervous:*** The phone costs a lot of money. ***The good news:*** Your friend has been talking about getting a new phone for a while.

Before you tell your parents about the test, maybe you can . . .

Reading

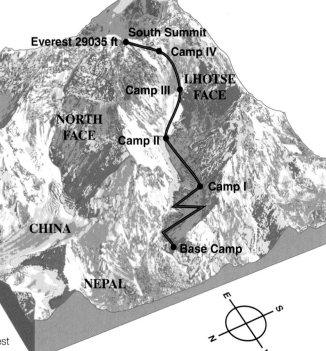

A climber's map of Mount Everest

A Complete the information about Mount Everest with numbers from the box. Then answer the questions with a partner.

200	60,000	8,850	1953

At 29,035 feet—(1) _____ meters—Mount Everest is the highest point on Earth. In (2) _____, New Zealander Edmund Hillary and Sherpa[1] Tenzing Norgay first reached the summit.[2] Although thousands of people from all over the world try to reach the summit each spring, it's not easy. Climbing Everest is risky: more than (3) _____ people have died on the mountain from snow, intense cold, and altitude[3] sickness. It's also expensive: guide services can cost up to (4) $_____ per person.

[1] **Sherpa** a local Nepalese climber who guides other climbers up Everest
[2] **summit** top [3] **altitude** height off the ground

- What are the risks and cost of climbing Mount Everest?
- Even though climbing Everest is dangerous, many people do it every year. Why do you think they do it?

B Read the title and the first two paragraphs of the article. Then answer the questions in your own words with a partner.

1. Who are Scott Fischer and Rob Hall?
2. How did Scott and Rob compete?
3. Was there any reason to worry about people climbing to the summit on May 10?
4. What do you think is going to happen next in the story?

C Read the rest of the article. How are these dates and times important to the story? Write a sentence or two about each on a separate piece of paper.

May 10   2:00 p.m.   3:00 p.m.   10:00 p.m.   May 11

D Summarize the story, using your answers in Exercises **B** and **C**.

Ask
Answer
Why do you think Rob and Scott didn't make their teams turn around at 2:00 p.m. on May 10? What lesson can we learn from this story?

MOUNT EVEREST'S
Deadliest Day

1 Climbing Mount Everest is dangerous business, but even so, tourists pay enormous sums of money to take the risk. In 1996, there were more fatalities on Mount Everest than any other year . . . and half of those people died on just one day.

Scott Fischer and Rob Hall made a living guiding people up the mountain, but they didn't work together. They each owned adventure companies, Adventure Consultants and Mountain Madness, that allowed people 10 to explore Mount Everest. Scott and Rob were good friends, but they were also rivals.[1] They each tried to get their groups to the summit first, and they often competed for clients. That May, both Scott and Rob decided that the 10th was the perfect day to set out for the summit. Scott's team had twenty three people in it, and Rob's had twenty five. There was also a twelve-person crew on Everest that day, making a movie about climbing the mountain. Consequently, there were more people trying to climb Mount Everest in May 1996 than at any other time 20 before. One member of the movie crew, Ed Viesturs, was good friends with Rob and Scott and was worried about safety with so many people climbing at the same time.

Rob's and Scott's teams set off[2] early on May 10th. They left for the summit of Mount Everest from camp 4. It was a beautiful day, with perfect weather. Ed was at camp 2 and was monitoring[3] the progress of the climbers using a radio and telescope. Ed looked through the telescope at around 2:00 p.m. to check on the climbers. He noticed 30 that the groups were moving

very slowly. It is a rule on Mount Everest that at 2:00 p.m. you are to turn around and return to camp 4 in order to make it back before dark and avoid bad weather near the summit. Rob and Scott each wanted their groups to reach the top, so both groups ignored that critical rule and continued up the mountain instead of turning around.

Suddenly, at 3:00 p.m. a massive snowstorm started. By 10:00 p.m. that night, people from both Rob's and Scott's groups were trapped on the mountain in between 40 the summit and camp 4 because of the storm. Some of

> Rob and Scott each wanted their groups to reach the summit, so both groups ignored that critical rule and continued up the mountain instead of turning around.

the stranded climbers managed to survive the freezing cold and were rescued from the mountain the next day. However, on May 11th a few others collapsed and died in the snow, including Scott Fischer and Rob Hall. In total, eight people died on Mount Everest's deadliest day.

[1] **rival** a person you compete with
[2] **set off** (for a place) to start a trip
[3] **monitor** to follow or check something regularly

Video

caught off guard to be surprised by someone or something	**sea level** on the ground, near the ocean
disorientation confusion	**soak (something) in** to look at or enjoy a place you are in as much as you can
oxygen a gas (O) in the air needed by humans to breathe	**zombie** a dead person who has come back to life

A Read the information below. Then ask a partner: How do you think climbing Everest has changed since 1996 when Rob Hall ran Adventure Consultants? Watch **segment 2** of the video to check your answer.

Adventure Consultants, originally owned by New Zealander Rob Hall, continues to guide people to the top of Everest. Today it is run by climber Guy Cotter. In the video, he's going to lead a Canadian group (nicknamed Team Canada) to the summit.

B Look back at the map on p. 54. Then watch **segment 3** of the video. Match a sentence stem (1–8) with an answer (a–g). Sometimes an answer can be used more than once.

Team Canada's Everest Expedition

1. Team Canada sets out on foot to base camp . . .
2. Today, Adventure Consultants uses computers and satellite phones . . .
3. At base camp, the team does the Puja ceremony . . .
4. For weeks, Team Canada travels back and forth between camps 1 to 4 . . .
5. In mid-May, the guides prepare supplemental oxygen . . .
6. The team stops at the fourth and final camp before the summit . . .
7. The team sets off the next morning for the summit . . .
8. They take some photos and look at the view . . .

   a. since they will need extra to survive on the mountain.
   b. before daybreak.
   c. because they need to adjust to the altitude.
   d. after they reach the top.
   e. so that they can rest.
   f. before they are allowed to climb the mountain.
   g. so that they can check the weather report.

C Watch the video again and check your answers in Exercise **B**.

During the Puja ceremony, climbers say prayers to Mother Goddess of the Earth (the Nepalese name for Everest).

D Use the map on p. 54 and your answers in Exercise **B** to explain Team Canada's Everest journey. How long was it from the start in April to the finish?

Ask

Answer What do you think of people who climb Everest? Would you do it? Why or why not?

Speaking

A Read the information below. What problem are people meeting to discuss?

Local business people, mountain climbers, and interested parties from around the world are debating closing Mount Everest. Some want to stop all climbing and camping for environmental and, above all, safety reasons. Others say that this will cause many people to lose their jobs. Should Everest be closed?

B Work in groups of four. Follow these steps and use the expressions in the Speaking Strategy to help you.

1. **Assign** each role from the box below to one person.
2. **Read** the information about your part <u>only</u>.
3. **Introduce** yourself and explain your opinion.
4. **On your own**, think of one or two possible solutions (close Everest completely; keep it open year round to everyone; something in-between). Try to think of a solution everyone can accept.
5. **Start the discussion**. One person suggests a possible solution and explains the reasoning. The others should then respond. Continue negotiating until you all agree on <u>one</u> solution.

Speaking Strategy	Reaching a compromise
	Making a suggestion
	One option / idea would be to . . .
	Another (option / idea) would be to . . .
	Disagreeing with a suggestion
	The problem with that is . . .
	Sorry, but that doesn't work for me because . . .
	Agreeing with a suggestion
	I could do that / agree to that.
	That works for me.
	Offering a compromise
	If you'll agree to . . . , I'll agree to . . .

Everest guide: You lead groups of international climbers up Mount Everest each spring. You employ nine people. Even though some of your clients are not fully trained to make the climb, none have ever been injured. However, you have recently almost had a couple of accidents, and you are not enjoying your work like you used to. If Everest closes, your business will collapse.

Mountain climber: You've been training to climb Everest for a year. It's your dream to reach the top, and you don't want the mountain to close. You've heard stories about inexperienced climbers being injured—or worse. You think these people should not be allowed on Everest.

Environmentalist: Everest gets thousands of visitors every year. The result: water and air pollution have increased. Climbers leave garbage on the mountain. There are also over a hundred dead bodies still on Everest. You believe the mountain must close so that it can be cleaned up and preserved for the future.

Local Sherpa guide: You've been a mountain guide for several years. Even though you make good money doing it, you're very concerned about safety. Your brother was also a trained guide. Last spring, though, he died in an avalanche* near the summit. In your opinion, something has to change.

C Explain your group's solution to the class.

> One option would be to close Everest for a year so that we can clean it . . .

*avalanche a large amount of snow that falls down a mountain

Writing
A Set of Instructions

A If you are swimming and you see a shark, what is the first thing you should do?

  a. Pretend you are dead.   b. Splash and attract attention.   c. Remain still.

B Read the information. Then answer the questions below with a partner.

Surviving a Shark Attack

Last summer, I was a lifeguard at a beach near my house. Before I started, I had to take a class. In it, I learned different water safety skills, including how to handle the situation if a shark attacked.

Although shark attacks are rare, they are very dangerous. If you see a shark while you're in the water, you should follow these steps. **The first is** to stay very still. Do not panic and start moving a lot because this will attract the shark. Also, do not pretend you are dead and assume the shark will just go away. Dead animals attract sharks! **The next thing you should do is** to get out of the water quickly and calmly. Don't splash around or attract attention. **While** you are moving toward the shore, keep watching for the shark so that it doesn't come back and surprise you. If the shark *does* come and attack, then **the only thing you can do is** to fight back. Hit the shark in the nose and eyes very hard. Because these are sensitive areas on the shark's body, it might scare the animal so that you can get away safely. **As soon as** you're out of the water, report the shark sighting right away. Following these steps can help you stay safe.

1. Was your guess in Exercise **A** correct?
2. What do the boldfaced words show the reader?
3. Close your book. Can you recall the instructions the lifeguard gave?

C Read the Writing Strategy. Then choose one of the topics below to write about.

Explain how to . . .

- tell someone bad news (pick something specific).
- improve your English conversation skills.
- prepare for an important exam.
- stay safe if there is a fire.
- your idea: _____

D Make a list of steps in the process. How is each step helpful? Then write a paragraph or two on a separate piece of paper.

E Exchange papers with another student. Read your partner's writing. Does it follow the Writing Strategy?

> **Writing Strategy**
>
> **Explaining steps in a process**
> When you describe how to do something, (1) identify specific steps in the process; (2) use signal words and phrases such as *first, next, then, last, when, while,* and *as soon as* to mark the steps. (See the boldfaced words in Exercise **B**.); and (3) briefly explain why each step in the process is helpful: *The first (thing you should do) is stay very still.* <u>*Do not panic and start moving a lot because this will attract the shark.*</u>

Expanding Your Fluency

A On your own, read the situation below. Then make an escape plan. Be prepared to explain the steps in your plan and why you think each step is a good idea.

You and a friend were on a sailing tour. During the trip, there was a storm and your boat sank. Luckily, you and your friend survived and were able to swim to a small island, but you are now trapped on it. What are you going to do?

The island

You're on a beach and the weather is hot. There's no fresh water, but there are lots of coconut trees. (Coconuts usually have drinkable water in them.)

You can see a tall mountain in the center of the island. There are no buildings or people on your side of the mountain. You don't know what's on the other side. You thought you saw smoke coming from there, but you aren't sure.

Your supplies

Before the boat sank, you saved your waterproof backpack. Inside you find matches, a small first-aid kit, a fork, a sharp knife, a spoon, and a cell phone with a GPS system. The cell phone works but it isn't getting any reception right now.

Your situation

During the storm, your boat was blown off course. Even though a rescue team will search for you, they might not know where to look.

One of you injured your leg in the ordeal. You can walk, but it's painful.

B Imagine that you and your partner are trapped on the island. Explain your plans to each other. Use the expressions on p. 57 to help you negotiate and create <u>one</u> escape plan together.

> One option is to hike to the other side of the island and see what's there.

> The problem is that I injured my leg and can't walk very well. Also, before we hike to the other side, we need to . . .

C Share your escape plan with the class. When all pairs have presented their plans, vote for the best one.

Check What You Know

Rank how well you can perform these outcomes on a scale of 1–5 (5 being the best).

_____ use adverbial clauses to talk about challenging situations

_____ reach a compromise

_____ explain steps in a process

_____ follow steps to get through a difficult situation

6 In Style

1 What is happening in this photo? Have you ever been to a place like this?

2 A trend is something that is popular or in style. Do you follow fashion trends? Why or why not?

3 What is more important to you when it comes to fashion: quality or price?

Unit Outcomes

In this unit, you will learn to:

• describe shopping habits and fashion preferences

• use adjective clauses to explain and define people and things

• react to other points of view

• present and defend an argument

Vocabulary

affordable reasonably priced, inexpensive
bargain to talk with someone to try to get a lower price on something
brand a type of product made by a particular company
browse to look around a shop casually
deal something good you buy, usually for a low price

discount a reduction in the usual price of something
goods products you buy
purchase to buy something
quality how good or bad something is
recommend to suggest to someone that a thing or person would be good or useful

Usage: *bargain* and *deal* *Bargain* can also be a noun and means the same thing as *deal*. *The shoes cost only $25. What a bargain/deal!*

deal *bad ~, fair ~, good ~ great~, real ~*

A Choose the expressions in 1–3 that best describe your shopping habits. Then explain your responses to a partner.

1. When I shop, I like to **take my time and browse / hurry up and buy what I need.**

2. I **occasionally / never** try to bargain to get a discount on something.

3. The most important thing to me is that my purchases are **high quality / affordable.**

B Read what Nadia says about the Dubai Shopping Festival.

1. Complete the profile with a word from the vocabulary list.

2. Then ask a partner: Would you like to shop there? Why or why not? How is it similar to or different from shopping where you live?

Best time to shop: *I (1) _____ going in the early morning or late evening so you can avoid the crowds. You can find the best deals late in the day. Also, many people speak English so you don't have to worry about communicating with the locals.*

Best place to browse: *A traditional marketplace, called a souk. You can buy a variety of (2) _____ there, including furniture, jewelry, food, and spices. Merchants typically start with a high price and then (3) _____ with you for a more affordable one.*

What makes it special: *Over three million people attend. Also, people who (4) _____ items during the festival are entered into a daily lottery. Winners receive cars, money, and even gold!*

I love shopping at the Dubai Shopping Festival. Every year, over forty shopping malls and stores join together in January and February to offer big discounts on everything from brand name clothing to high-quality electronics and cars.

Ask

Answer In your city, is there a time of year when stores offer big discounts on goods? Do you ever shop at these sales?

Grammar

A Complete 1–3 with the correct word(s). Explain your answers to a partner.

1. People **who / which / that** enter the lottery can win prizes.
2. Did you buy the jacket **who / which / that** was on sale?
3. Dubai's traditional souks, **who / which / that** sell many goods, are very interesting.

Adjective Clauses with Subject Relative Pronouns

who = for people	❶ People **who visit Dubai during the shopping festival** can get some great deals.
which = for things	❷ The festival, **which gets over three million visitors**, lasts several weeks.
that = for people and things	❸ Nadia is someone **that spends a lot on clothes**. ❹ It's a festival **that takes place every year**.
subject-verb agreement	❺ It's a <u>shop</u> **that <u>sells</u>** discount electronics. ❻ They're <u>shops</u> **that <u>sell</u>** designer handbags.

Adjective clauses give more information about a noun and begin with a relative pronoun (*who, which, that*).
In ❶, the adjective clause gives <u>necessary information</u> about the subject. It completes the meaning of the sentence.
In ❷, the adjective clause gives <u>extra information</u> about the subject. You don't need it to complete the meaning of the sentence. It is separated from the main clause by commas.

 TIP When an adjective clause gives extra information, *that* cannot be used: *The festival, ~~that~~ which gets over three million visitors . . .*

 TIP Don't repeat the subject after the relative pronoun: *He's a person who ~~he~~ spends a lot on clothes.*

B Correct the mistake in each sentence. Then check your answers with a partner. In which sentences do the adjective clauses give necessary information? Which give extra information?

1. Men which live in Europe spend more money on clothes than men in North America.
2. Clothing and books are the most popular products that they are sold online.
3. Most people who lives in South Korea have purchased something online at least once.
4. The Bugatti Veyron, who is the most expensive car in the world, costs almost $2,500,000.
5. The Dubai Mall, that is one of the largest in the world, has over 1,200 stores.

C Combine the sentences using an adjective clause to form a single question. Then take turns asking and answering the questions with a partner.

Which shops have good bargains? I want something near here.
Which shops that are near here have good bargains?

1. Have you ever bought something? It was really expensive.
2. Can you name any clothing designers? They are known around the world.
3. Do you have any friends? They are very stylish.
4. Can you recommend a good place for vacation? It's fun and affordable.

 PRONUNCIATION Notice the different meaning and intonation patterns in these two examples.

The shopkeeper who sells such beautiful goods will make a lot of money.
The shopkeeper, who sells such beautiful goods, will make a lot of money.
For more information on intonation patterns in relative clauses, see p. 149.

Listening

A Where can you get good deals on electronics, clothes, and other goods? Have you ever purchased anything in one of these places? What did you buy? Discuss with a partner.

B You're going to hear three different conversations happening in Robson Street, a popular shopping district in Vancouver, Canada. Read the information below. Then listen and choose the correct answers.

a tablet

Conversation 1

1. The man and woman are looking at a tablet. The man _____.
   a. tells the woman not to buy it   b. bargains with the woman for it
   c. recommends another product

2. Does the woman purchase the tablet?   **Yes**   Price: _____   **No**   Why not: _____

Conversation 2

3. The woman who is shopping for shoes wants _____.
   a. evening shoes   b. reasonably priced shoes
   c. shoes like her friend's

4. Does the woman purchase any shoes?   **Yes**   Price: _____   **No**   Why not: _____

Conversation 3

5. The man _____.
   a. can't decide which bike to buy   b. bargains with the saleswoman
   c. is confused about the prices

6. Does the man purchase a bike?   **Yes**   Price: _____   **No**   Why not: _____

C Read the sentences below. Then listen again. Choose the correct answer for each one.

1. When the man says, "What a *rip off*!," he means "What a **cheap / high** price!"
2. When the woman says, "*Check out* this pair," she means, "**Look at / Forget about** these shoes."
3. When the woman says, "*It's worth it*," she means, "The bike is **cheap / expensive** because its quality is **good / bad**."

D Imagine that you are at the mall with your partner. Create a short dialog in which you use at least two of the new expressions from Exercise **C**. Then perform your dialog for another pair.

Vancouver, Canada

Connections

A Two people are bargaining at a flea market. Listen to and read the dialog. What's special about the pen the man is selling? Would you buy this product?

Buyer: This is an interesting looking pen. How much do you want for it?

Seller: $20.

Buyer: For this old pen?!

Seller: Ah, but it's not just *any* old pen. It's a pen that never runs out of ink.

Buyer: A pen that never runs out of ink? Really?

Seller: Yes. It's perfect for the person who never wants to buy another pen again! But I've only got three left. They're selling fast.

Buyer: Hmmm . . . Well, it *is* pretty . . . and you say it'll never run out of ink? I'll give you $5 for it.

Seller: Ten. Come on; think of all the money you'll save. Ten is a great deal.

Buyer: Six. That's all I can afford.

Seller: Six it is!

The Estremoz flea market in Portugal.

B You're going to sell an item at a flea market. Do the following:

1. Think of an everyday item (cell phone, watch, umbrella, article of clothing). Then give it a "special power." Answer the questions to describe your special item:
   - What does it do? It's a _____ that _____.
   - Who is it perfect for? It's perfect for people who _____.

> At a flea market, people sell old or used goods. You can often find odd objects, fantastic deals, and . . . a lot of junk!

2. Take four small pieces of paper. On each, write the item you listed in step 1. This paper now represents your merchandise. You are going to sell four of the same items at the flea market.

3. Decide on a cost for the item. It cannot be more than $100.

C Your instructor will divide the class into sellers and buyers. Read your information below.

Sellers	Buyers
Your goal: To sell all four of your items for as much money as you can before time is up.	**Your goal:** To buy as many products as you can before time is up. You start with $100 to spend.
Talk to different customers at the market. Explain what your item is and why it's useful. When you sell an item, give the paper to the buyer and add the amount you earned below.	Talk to different sellers. If you want to buy a product, bargain for a lower price. When you buy an item, deduct the amount you paid below. Also write the price on the paper the seller gives you.
Starting amount: 0	Starting amount: 100
+ _____ + _____ + _____ + _____	– _____ – _____ – _____ – _____ – _____ – _____ – _____ – _____
Total earned: _____	**Total left:** _____

D Start the bargaining! You will have fifteen minutes to buy or sell as many items as you can. When time is up, share your results with the class. Who were the most successful bargainers?

E Switch roles (those who were sellers are now buyers) and repeat Exercises **C** and **D**.

Reading

A The adjectives below are used to describe people. Mark the ones you know. Look up the ones you don't know in your dictionary. Then circle the ones that describe you.

adventurous	fashion-conscious	self-confident
daring	outgoing	serious
dependable	practical	sophisticated

B Read the title and the first paragraph of the article on the next page. Then look at the photos and ask a partner: Who might wear each pair of shoes? What can you tell about each person by looking at only his or her shoes?

C What does each type of shoe tell us about a person? Read the article and then complete the chart with information from the reading.

high-heeled shoes or boots for women	low-heeled or flat shoes for women
heavy boots for men	**designer shoes for men**
bright, multi-colored shoes	**neutral or darker colored shoes**
worn sneakers	**designer sneakers**

D How much can you tell about your partner by looking at his or her shoes? Describe him or her using the information in Exercise **C** to help you. Then share your description with your partner. Was it correct?

Every Shoe Tells a Story

A Christian Louboutin stiletto

1 Humans have been wearing shoes for thousands of years. They protect our feet from the heat and cold; they allow us to walk comfortably or to run faster. Our shoes do more than this, though. They can also tell others a lot about us. If your shoes could talk, what would they say about you?

Boy or girl?

One of the first things your shoes tell others about you is your gender. A high-heeled shoe, for example, probably belongs to a woman. This kind of shoe wasn't always
10 associated with[1] women, though. For hundreds of years, wealthy men and women in Europe and Asia wore high-heeled sandals or boots to protect their feet and clothes from mud and water on the ground.

Though today's streets are cleaner, 4- to 5-inch stilettos are still very popular among women. Beautiful? Perhaps. Practical? Not really. So why do so many women continue to wear them? Natacha Marro, who has designed shoes for pop stars like Christina Aguilera, explains. "You put on heels, and suddenly you are
20 6 inches [15 centimeters] higher. It's a power thing." Wearing stilettos (or any high-heeled shoe or boot) tells others that you're daring and self-confident. Some people find that very attractive. Low-heeled or flat shoes, on the other hand, project a more serious image. They tell others that you're practical and dependable.

What do you do?

For hundreds of years, shoes also told others about a person's occupation or social position. In early Japan, for example, merchants, actors, and soldiers wore shoes
30 specific to their line of work. Although we usually can't tell what a person does by looking at his or her shoes anymore, we can still make some guesses. A man who wears heavy boots on the job, for example, may work outside; perhaps he's a construction worker or firefighter. A man with a closet full of designer shoes, however, may need to dress more formally at work. Perhaps he's an attorney or business executive. Or maybe he just has the money to buy a lot of expensive shoes.

What are you like?

40 In ancient Rome, the wealthy could be identified by the red or orange shoes they wore. Though shoe color no longer indicates[2] one's social status, it does still tell us something about the shoe owner's personality. Bright, multi-colored shoes or those with lots of details suggest an outgoing, adventurous character. Neutral or darker colors, on the other hand, signal sophistication and self-control. Even the sneakers we wear can tell others a lot about us. A worn[3] pair, for example, suggests that you're a bit of a rebel—a person who doesn't care what
50 others think. A pair of $400 designer sneakers, however, tells others you're a fashion-conscious person who is interested in the latest trends, whatever the cost.

Our shoes say a lot about us, even when we aren't wearing them. Look at the shoes you've got on right now. What do they tell others about you?

[1] **associated with** to be connected or related to another thing
[2] **indicate** to show
[3] **worn** old, damaged, used a lot

Video

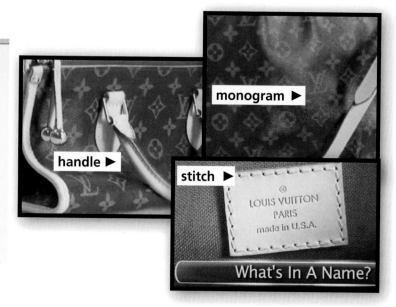

authentic real, genuine

canvas a type of strong, heavy cloth, used for making clothes and bags

crooked not straight; bent or curved

dealer someone who sells something

fake not real

imitator someone who copies what someone else does

instinct your feeling about something

spot to identify

handle ▶

monogram ▶

stitch ▶

® LOUIS VUITTON PARIS made in U.S.A.

What's In A Name?

A Discuss the questions with a partner.

1. Do you ever see people selling fake designer goods? What kinds? Why do you think fake goods are so popular?

2. Look at the photos of the handbags. Can you guess which one is real and which is fake? How?

B Read the title of the video. In pairs, try to guess the answers in steps 1–5. Then watch the video once through—without writing anything—to check your ideas.

How to Spot a Fake Louis Vuitton Bag

Step 1: The price is (a.) _____.

• Most bags sell for over (b.) $ _____. If you pay less than $300 for a new bag, you're not getting a deal, you're getting a (c.) _____.

Step 2: Usually the "LVs" on a fake bag are (d.) _____.

• If you have any LVs that are in a crease or in a (e.) _____, it is not the real thing.

Step 3: The color of the leather handles should be a light (f.) _____, with the edge dyed (g.) _____ and the stitching in (h.) _____.

• After a few weeks, the handles should change to a darker (i.) _____. If they don't, the bag is a fake.

Step 4: If you buy a Louis Vuitton bag from a street (j.) _____, it's not genuine.

• You should also be careful about buying bags (k.) _____.

• Pay attention to seller feedback and ask about buyer protection and the (l.) _____ policy.

Step 5: Trust your (m.) _____.

• If you feel funny about (n.) _____ you're paying, walk away.

C Watch the video again and complete the first sentence in steps 1–5 in Exercise **B**. Then watch it again and complete the rest of the blanks.

D In addition to designer clothing and accessories, other fake goods sold worldwide include music, movies, car parts, computer software, electronics, and even food and medicine. Would you ever buy any of these goods? Why or why not? Discuss with a partner.

Speaking

A On your own and on a separate piece of paper, complete statements 1–4 with your opinion.

Shopping and Fashion: What Do You Think?

1. I think people who buy designer goods …
2. I think people who always dress casually …
3. I think men who wear …
4. I think women that wear …

B Get into a group of three people and do the following:

1. Take four small pieces of paper and write a number (1, 2, 3, 4) on each one. Then shuffle them and place them face down on the desk.
2. One person starts by picking up a number. Read your corresponding sentence from Exercise **A** aloud and explain your reasons to the group.
3. The other people in the group should then use the expressions in the Speaking Strategy below to agree or disagree with the statement and each other. When you state an opinion, remember to explain your reasons.
4. Return the number to the pile and then it is another person's turn. Repeat steps 1–3 until everyone has shared all of their sentences from Exercise **A**.

> I think people who buy designer goods are probably rich. You need a lot of money to afford those things.

> I'm not so sure about that. I know someone who owns several pairs of designer shoes and she isn't rich; she just likes high-quality goods.

Speaking Strategy

Expressing strong agreement
I couldn't agree (with you) more.
Yeah, no question / doubt about it.

Questioning another's point of view
I don't know / I'm not so sure about that.
I guess so, but at the same time . . .
I see / know / understand what you're saying . . . but don't you think . . .

Expressing strong disagreement
I completely disagree.
Are you kidding? (Informal)
No way! (Informal)
Informal phrases can sound rude. Only use these when you strongly disagree and with someone you know well.

Writing

Present and Defend an Argument

A Read the paragraphs. Then complete the steps below with a partner.

I think selling fake goods is wrong. Some people might disagree with this opinion, but I believe there are two important reasons why I'm right. First, people who sell fake goods, or "knockoffs," are stealing money from the original product manufacturer.* This is not fair. Of course, <u>many people who buy fakes say</u> they can't afford to pay full price for name brands. **While that may be true**, buying or selling fake goods is still a form of stealing and it is wrong.

TIP Stating an opposite opinion and explaining why you think it is weak can help support your argument.

Second, people who sell knockoffs sometimes trick buyers into purchasing something. These days, there are lots of Web sites that sell fake products as "the real thing." Shoppers think they are buying a designer handbag or MP3 player at a discounted price. In reality, they are buying a knockoff, but they don't know it. <u>A lot of people think</u> it's easy to spot fake goods because the quality is poor or the brand name is different. **However**, it's often hard to tell the difference between fake and real items that are sold online. For these reasons, I think selling fake goods is wrong.

*__manufacturer__ maker

1. List the writer's main argument (paragraph 1) in the chart below.
2. The writer gives two reasons to support the argument. Write the second one under "reasons."
3. He also states two opposite opinions from other people. What are they?

The main argument: _____

Reasons	Opposite opinions
1. *People who sell fake goods are stealing money from the original manufacturer.*	1. *Most people can't afford to pay full price for designer items.*
2.	2.

B Read the sentence and follow the steps below:

I **think / don't think** buying designer brands is a good way to spend your money.

1. Circle the word(s) in the sentence that express your opinion.
2. On a separate piece of paper, create a chart like the one in Exercise **A**. List two reasons to support your argument. Also think of an opposite opinion for each of your reasons.

Writing Strategy

Making a successful argument When you argue a point, you should . . .

• clearly state what your opinion is. Are you for or against something?
• give reasons that support your opinion.
• include opposite opinions using expressions like the ones underlined in the sample. You should also show why you disagree with those opinions using expressions like the ones in bold in Exercise **A**.

C Write two or three short paragraphs that argue your point, using the information in your chart.

D Exchange papers with another student. Read your partner's writing. Does your partner successfully follow the Writing Strategy?

Expanding Your Fluency

A Read the short passage. Then answer the questions with a partner.

You've been to sales at department stores. You've purchased things online at discount prices. Perhaps you've even visited a flea market and found a few bargains. But have you ever shopped at a store where everything was *free*? Stores like this have existed for years all over the world, and today they are growing in popularity.

How does a free store work? People bring in goods that they don't use anymore: clothing, electronics, bikes, furniture, art, jewelry, books, music. The items must be good quality; they can't be old, worn, dirty, or broken. People who come into the store can also take anything they want—without paying for it. A free store isn't only for those who can't afford to buy new things, though. The goal of these stores is to encourage *all* people to reuse items, not to throw them away or to keep buying new stuff all the time.

1. What is a free store and how does it work?   2. Who shops at a free store?

B Complete the sentences with your opinions. Think of two reasons to support each opinion.

1. I think a free store **would / wouldn't** be a good addition to my neighborhood because. . . .
2. I think everyone **should / shouldn't** be allowed to shop in a free store because. . . .

C Discuss your opinions in pairs. Use the expressions in the Speaking Strategy on p. 69 to agree or disagree with each other.

Check What You Know

Rank how well you can perform these outcomes on a scale of 1–5 (5 being the best).

_____ describe shopping habits and fashion preferences
_____ use adjective clauses to explain and define people and things
_____ react to other points of view
_____ present and defend an argument

7 On the Move

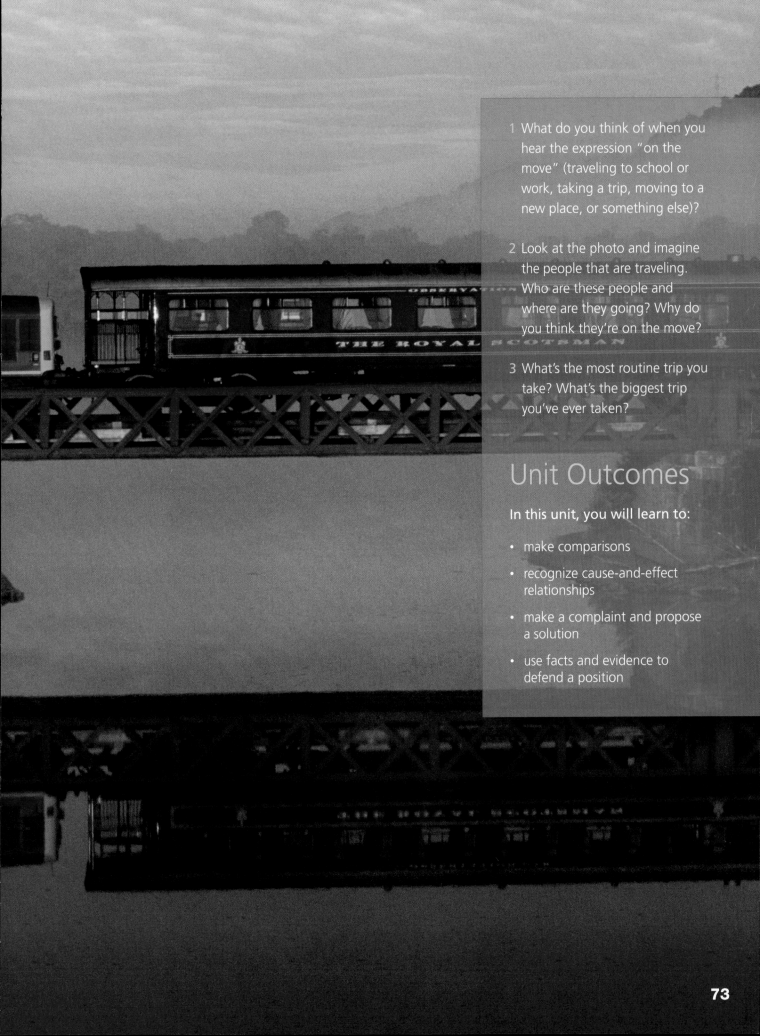

1 What do you think of when you hear the expression "on the move" (traveling to school or work, taking a trip, moving to a new place, or something else)?

2 Look at the photo and imagine the people that are traveling. Who are these people and where are they going? Why do you think they're on the move?

3 What's the most routine trip you take? What's the biggest trip you've ever taken?

Unit Outcomes

In this unit, you will learn to:

- make comparisons

- recognize cause-and-effect relationships

- make a complaint and propose a solution

- use facts and evidence to defend a position

Vocabulary

A How do people get around where you live—by bike, car, train? Make a list of all the modes of transportation (including walking). Then answer these questions with a partner.

Which mode of transportation is best when you . . .

1. are going to work or school?　　2. want to take a long trip?　　3. don't have a lot of money?

---

commute the daily journey you make between your home and work or school

cramped not big enough for the number of people or things in it

delay when you have to wait longer than expected for something to happen

fit in to feel that you belong to a particular group and are accepted by them

keep in mind to remember something important (often a warning / advice)

option something you can choose from a group of alternatives

overwhelming difficult to fight against

punctual on time; not late

reliable trusted to work or behave well

rush hour the times of day when most people are traveling to and from work

tend likely to behave in a particular way

transfer to go or move something from one place to another

> Other expressions with *keep*: *~ your promise/ word, ~ an appointment, ~ a secret, ~ up*

B Read Vanessa's tips about getting around her city. Use words from the list above to complete her advice.

Getting around a big city can be (1) _____. There are so many transportation (2) _____ that it's hard to know which one to choose. Here's my advice. When you have to travel a long distance, think twice before getting into a taxi. They can be expensive, and heavy traffic can result in frequent (3) _____. Take the subway instead. It may not always be (4) _____, but it's reasonably priced, clean, and reliable. You should (5) _____, though, that most locals use the subway to commute to and from work or school. Allow extra time if you have several transfers to make. If you don't like cramped spaces, it's best to avoid the subway during (6) _____. For short trips, you can simply walk to your destination. If you do all these things, you'll fit in just like a local!

C How does your city or town compare to Vanessa's? Work with a partner to complete these sentences.

1. When you have to go a long distance, you should . . .
2. For short trips, it's best to . . .
3. When it comes to commuting, most locals . . .
4. The best way to avoid delays is to . . .
5. The most important thing to keep in mind is . . .

Grammar

A Compared to five years ago, which of these sentences describes rush hour in your city or town today? Complete the sentences with the correct comparative form of *convenient*. Then choose an answer.

a. It's _____ to get around than it was before. (It's better.)

b. It's _____ than it was before. (It's worse.)

c. It's about the same.

> ⚙ **TIP** We don't usually use *less* with one-syllable adjectives. We use *not as . . . as* instead. ~~The bus is less fast than the train.~~ *The bus is not as fast as the train.*

Comparative Forms

	more than . . .	less than . . .	equal to . . .
Adjectives	Taking a taxi is **faster** and **more reliable than** taking the subway.	The subways are **less reliable than** they used to be. They are **not as nice as** they once were.	During rush hour, walking is **as fast as** taking the bus.
Adverbs	The trains run **faster** and **more frequently** than the bus.	The trains run **less frequently** on weekends than they do on weekdays.	The old trains run **as smoothly as** the new ones.
Noncount nouns	After I quit, I had **more time than** I used to.	As a new parent, I have **less time than** I used to.	I spend **as much** time working **as** (I did) before.
Count nouns	The local train makes **more stops than** the express (does).	The express train makes **fewer stops than** the local (does).	The Blue Line has **as many riders** as it did last year.
Irregular forms: good → better, bad → worse, far → further			

B Make sentences comparing these two subway lines. Which would you prefer to ride?

	Blue Line	Green Line
number of riders	140,000 per month	100,000 per month
train tracks	2 years old	15 years old
daily schedule	weekdays: every 5 minutes weekend: every 16 minutes	weekdays: every 5 minutes weekends: every 12 minutes
on time schedule	arrives late 8% of the time	arrives late 2% of the time
cleanliness	moderately clean	very clean
hear the announcements	clear 97% of the time	clear 82% of the time

C You are going to talk about the best way to travel between two points. Work with a group.

1. Choose a starting point and an ending point in a place you know well. The points should be far enough apart to require a combination of public transportation, driving, or walking to get there.

2. Think of two different routes you could take to get to your final destination.

3. Compare the pros and cons of the two routes using comparative language.

Listening

A Look at the photo below. How long is your typical commute to school or work?

B Listen to a news broadcast in which the reporter, Jeremy Wexler, talks about his commute. As you listen, mark the correct answer for each item.

1. The average commuting time is **increasing / decreasing**.
2. Jeremy probably lives in **the suburbs / the city**.
3. It is **common / not common** for the 8:12 train to be late.
4. His office is **near / far from** the train station.
5. He's probably **sitting / standing** on the train.
6. Jeremy takes **one train / more than one train** to work.

Listening Strategy **Connecting ideas** Listen for expressions like these that connect ideas. They show a cause-and-effect relationship between one idea and another: *As a result . . . / Because of that . . . / That means that . . . / When that happens . . .*

C Read the Listening Strategy. Then listen again. Mark your answers to show the cause-and-effect relationships that Jeremy describes.

1. The trains are **older / newer**. → They break down **more / less** often. → They run **more / less** frequently. → People are **more / less** likely to find a seat.
2. The stations are **cleaner / not as clean**. → The commute is **more / less** pleasant.
3. Traffic is **better / worse** these days. → Commuting by car is **slower / faster**.

Ask

Answer Central Station seems to be the busiest commuting hub in Jeremy's city. What about your city or town? What is the busiest center for transportation? How does it compare to Central Station?

Video

availability the fact that something can be used or reached

bottom line the total amount of money a company has made or lost over a particular amount of time

perfect match two things that go or work together successfully

A Read about bikeshare programs. Is there anything like this where you live?

Bikeshare programs provide bicycles for public use as an alternative to driving or taking public transportation. For a small fee, individuals can join the program and use the bicycles for short trips around the city. There are currently about two hundred bikeshare programs worldwide.

> **Word Partnership**
>
> Look at the verbs in blue. What do they mean? Use your dictionary to help you.
>
> I use bikeshare to **get around** town.
>
> I **get on** the bike near the station and **drop** it **off** ten minutes later.
>
> I use bikeshare when I have to **pick up** my son at school.

B Washington, DC is the capital of the United States. The city has a bikeshare program. Follow these steps.

   a. Read through items 1–6 below. Can you guess any of the answers?

   b. Watch the video once. Don't write anything.

   c. Watch again and complete the sentences.

1. **Chris Holbern:** Bikesharing works well in _____ areas. There are 114 _____ and 1,100 bikes. You can join for a year, a _____, or a day. Bikesharing is not only open to residents but _____ too.

2. **Matt Pearson:** The program is great for _____ and it brings more people to the _____ area.

3. **Chris:** The bike has _____ speeds, a basket, a bell, and a _____ for use at night.

4. **Matt:** The bikes are not only safe but _____ too.

5. **Chris:** We have to keep the system _____ and fix the bikes. When a station gets too full, we have a _____ that picks up bikes and transfers them to another _____ .

6. **Matt:** Businesses think that bikeshare has improved their _____ _____ .

C Read the sentences. Then listen to each speaker in the video and choose the correct answer.

1.   2.   3.   4.

MELEAH GEERTSMA
Capital Bikeshare User

5.

SHIN-PEI TSAY
Long Distance Commuter

_____ **a.** Bikesharing helped me to lose weight.

_____ **b.** I don't worry about anyone stealing my bike.

_____ **c.** I use bikeshare day or night when I'm visiting Washington.

_____ **d.** You can check ahead to see if any bikes are available.

_____ **e.** A lot of professional people like me use bikeshare.

Ask

Answer Would you use bikeshare? What are some of the disadvantages of a bikesharing program?

Connections

A Read the description of a bikesharing program in Exercise **A** on page 77. Would it work in your city or town? Why or why not?

B Read the facts about the bikesharing program. Then read about Henry's and Giovanni's opinions on bikesharing. Add one more item to each person's list.

> Bikesharing program, FACTS
> * Membership costs $90 a year.
> * Helmets are not provided.
> * Five hundred single-speed bikes are available.

Henry

I support bikesharing. I think we should introduce a bikesharing system in my city.

The bikesharing system . . .

— gives you an easy and reliable way to get around town.
— promotes sustainable transportation.
— is a good option when the subways are delayed.
— is easy to navigate—anyone can use it.
— saves you time between transfers.
— means you can avoid cramped subway cars.
— _____.

Giovanni

I'm against bikesharing. I think we should lower the fares and encourage people to use the subway.

The bikesharing system . . .

— will take taxpayer money to maintain and take money away from other transportation projects.
— will overwhelm the streets with too many bikes.
— doesn't provide helmets for riders and therefore puts people's lives at risk.
— is not suitable for long-distance trips.
— is not affordable for some people.
— _____.

C Do a role-play.

Student A: You agree with Henry. Explain why you support bikesharing. Compare it to riding the subway.

Student B: You agree with Giovanni. Explain why you are against bikesharing. Compare it to riding the subway.

> Bikesharing is a good idea. For shorter distances, it's faster than waiting for a bus or the subway.

> It may be faster in some cases, but it's not as safe. Keep in mind that bikesharing will put more bicyclists on the road. As a result . . .

Writing

A Letter of Complaint

A   What would you do if bus and subway fares increased two times in one year?

☐ **1.** Call or e-mail my complaint to the city.   ☐ **3.** Just accept it and do nothing.

☐ **2.** Complain to my family and friends about how unfair it is.

B   Read Joanna's letter of complaint. Then answer the questions with a partner.

> Dear Representative Meyer,
>
> Recently you voted against a bikesharing plan for our city. I'm writing to ask that you support it.
>
> As a commuter on the Blue Line, I used to transfer from the subway to the B41 bus to get to my office. As you know, because of the weak economy, there have been transportation cuts. As a result, the B41 bus line has been eliminated, and I have no reliable way to get to work easily.
>
> The distance between the subway station and my office is too far to walk. A cab is one option, but taking a taxi is expensive. I'm feeling very frustrated by this situation.
>
> A bikesharing system would not only be good for the city (fewer people riding in cars means less pollution), but it's also convenient for someone like me: I need to travel between the subway and my office quickly and safely, and riding a bike would be the perfect solution for me!
>
> Thank you for your attention to this matter,   Joanna O'Shea

 TIP State your request up front. Present the problem. Show cause and effect where possible.

 TIP Offer a solution and explain how it helps.

1. Who is the letter written to?
2. What's Joanna's problem?
3. What caused it?
4. What's her solution?

C   Think of a problem you'd like to see changed. Choose from the problems below or use your own idea. On a separate piece of paper, write notes about the problem, its causes, and a solution.

If you live in a city, write about . . .

- the increasing cost of public transportation
- traffic congestion
- cuts in transportation services

If you live in a town, write about . . .

- the lack of a subway or bus system
- poor transportation options to nearby towns
- the lack of easy access to a major airport

D   Write a letter of complaint using your notes. Be sure to use the writing tips. Then exchange papers with another student. Read your partner's letter. Does it do the three things on the Writing Checklist? Do you think the request will be granted? Why or why not?

Writing Checklist

Does the letter . . .

1. state the writer's request clearly?
2. explain what the problem is and what caused it?
3. offer a possible solution?

Reading

A Read the statistics below and then ask your partner:
How does your country compare to the ones in the chart? Do many people from other nations come to live in your country permanently or temporarily? If so, where do they come from?

People all over the globe are on the move, with many moving permanently or temporarily to a country other than their own.

Country	% of the population that is foreign-born
Canada	18.7%
India	0.5%
Singapore	42.6%
Germany	12.3%

B Read the article. What is the main point of this article?

a. The parents and students disagree over cars and driving rules.

b. All students dream about getting away and going somewhere fun.

c. The student body is diverse, but they all share an interest in cars.

d. The students' diverse backgrounds help them to get a driver's license.

C Quickly find and underline the answers to questions 1–6 in the reading. Then take turns asking and answering them with a partner.

1. How old do the students need to be to get a license?
2. Why do they want a car?
3. Where do they want to go?
4. What kind of car do they want?
5. What kind of car do their parents want them to drive?
6. What are some of the rules they have to follow?

D Look at these ideas from the reading about driving. What do you think they mean? Which ones do you agree with?

1. "Your car is your life."
2. "Doesn't everyone want to get away?"
3. "The teens want a new car that makes a statement."

Ask
Answer   In the United States, a driver's first car symbolizes independence and adulthood. Does driving have the same meaning for you? What symbolizes independence in your culture?

ONE FOOT on the GAS

Everyone has a backpack. Boys tend to wear jeans and T-shirts; girls wear skirts or pants. Boys and girls wear earrings and talk about the same music. To an outsider, it looks like just another typical day at J.E.B. Stuart High School.

But running beneath the common fashion and attitude[1] are their cultural differences at home: many of the students have parents who came to the United States from other countries. Walking through the halls of Stuart, one meets students from a variety of different backgrounds: an African American, an Afghan Italian, a Cambodian, and a Palestinian. The students take pride in their diversity even as they try to fit in as everyday American teenagers.

Conversations, especially among the boys, quickly turn to cars. "A car means freedom," one says. "You can go anywhere—your car is your life." One boy, who is saving his part-time job earnings[2] for a car, says, "With a car I could go with my friends to the beach or to New York. Life in general can get overwhelming sometimes. Doesn't everyone want to get away?"

And get away they do. Teenagers in many states in the United States can get a license at the age of 16 and most are eager to start driving right away. Teen drivers have a higher rate of road accidents, however. Because of that, the student drivers at Stuart will have to follow their parents' rules: No talking or texting on your cell phone while driving. Remember to wear your seat belt.

Don't drive too fast. Commuting to school is all right, but driving in the city's rush hour is not allowed. When taking the car out, remember to bring it home on time. Being safe, reliable, and punctual is important, say parents.

For most new drivers, it's important for a car to be attractive and cool: They want a new car that can "make a statement." Their parents, on the other hand, are looking for a car for their child that is economical, affordable, and most of all, safe. As a result, most teens start driving with the family car that's available—which is usually the oldest, least attractive one of the bunch.

Back at Stuart High, at 2:05 p.m., the school day ends, and a rush to buses and cars begins. Some students get rides with parents or friends. Others get to drive themselves. Music blares[3] from car radios and the kids who are left behind sit on the grass talking, laughing, and just hanging out with friends.

These are normal American teenagers whose parents happen to come from all over the world. They may have one foot in their parents' culture, but they share one thing with their US-born classmates: They all have one foot on the gas pedal . . . and they are ready to go!

[1] **attitude** the way you think and feel about something
[2] **earnings** the money you make while working
[3] **blare** to make a loud, unpleasant sound

Speaking

A Read this information about Amadou and his parents. Then discuss the questions with a partner.

- Amadou is a first-year college student studying urban planning and transportation. He's an excellent student.

- His parents are from the Republic of Mali. They came to your country with Amadou when he was 2 years old.

- His parents have been working in your country for years without the proper work visas.

- Three months ago, Amadou was stopped for speeding in his car and the police realized he didn't have the proper papers.

- The government wants to send Amadou and his parents back to Mali because they are in the country illegally.

- Amadou wants to stay in your country, finish his education, and get a job.

- Amadou hasn't lived in Mali since he was a baby and he doesn't speak the language.

In your opinion, what should happen? Should Amadou be allowed to stay?

B Get into a group of three people. Two students will be attorneys (one supporting Amadou's position, the other against it). The other student will be a judge. Follow the steps below:

1. **Attorneys for and against Amadou:** Read the arguments below. Together, add one or two more reasons to your list. Also think about how you will address the arguments the other attorney presents.

   Judges: Read the arguments below. Together, add one or two more reasons. Also think about how you will address the arguments the attorneys will present.

Why Amadou should stay	Why Amadou should go
1. Amadou only knows this country. If he has to leave now, he may miss the chance to finish his education and have a better life.	1. The law is clear. Amadou's family broke the law when they entered your country on tourist visas and stayed on. They must all leave.
2. Amadou and his parents have worked hard and have never been in trouble with the law.	2. If you allow Amadou to stay in your country, many other foreigners will try to do the same thing.
3. Amadou did nothing wrong. He was brought to your country as a baby.	3. The economy is doing poorly, and many people are unemployed. Amadou and his parents will take jobs away from legal residents.
4. Last year, the government gave special work permits to 200 undocumented foreigners.	4. _____ 5. _____
5. _____ 6. _____	

2. **Begin the role-play.** The attorneys will argue their case for or against Amadou. The judges will listen to each point and can ask questions at any time. Use the Speaking Strategy to help you.

3. **Make a decision.** At the end, the judges should review their notes, consider the attorneys' arguments, and make a decision about Amadou's future. They should then explain their ruling.

> **Speaking Strategy**
>
> ***Presenting facts*** When making an argument, it is important to support your position with facts and evidence.
>
> **Considering that/Given that** Amadou's parents broke the law . . .
>
> **Keeping in mind (that)** Amadou doesn't want to be separated . . .
>
> **If you think about it**, Amadou only knows life in this country . . .
>
> ***Announcing your decision*** To show that you are making a fair, informed decision, acknowledge that you have heard and understood all the facts presented.
>
> **When I look at all the options**, it's clear that . . .
>
> **After weighing all the options / factors**, I have decided . . .
>
> **After much consideration**, . . .

Expanding Your Fluency

Read these statements. Then join a partner and follow the steps below.

Talk about . . .

- the worst commute you ever had
- the first time you drove a car / flew in a plane / took a train
- the longest distance you've ever traveled
- your favorite car and why you like it
- why you would or wouldn't like to join a bikeshare program
- the best way to get around your city or town
- the worst thing about owning a car

1. Flip a coin to decide who goes first (Student **A**). **A** picks a statement and talks about it for a minute without stopping.
2. **B** goes next and can choose any statement except for the one that **A** already talked about.
3. Take turns talking for a minute until all the statements have been chosen once.
4. Award one point when a person can talk successfully for one minute without stopping. The winner is the person with the most points at the end.

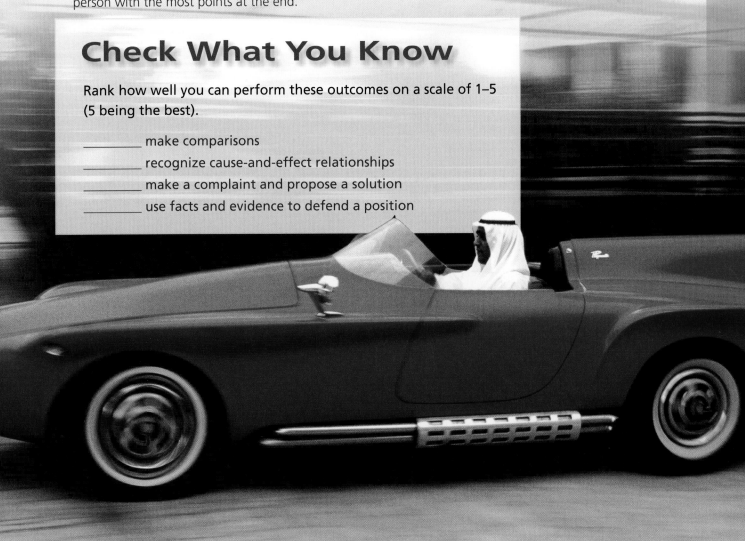

Check What You Know

Rank how well you can perform these outcomes on a scale of 1–5 (5 being the best).

_____ make comparisons

_____ recognize cause-and-effect relationships

_____ make a complaint and propose a solution

_____ use facts and evidence to defend a position

8 Think Twice

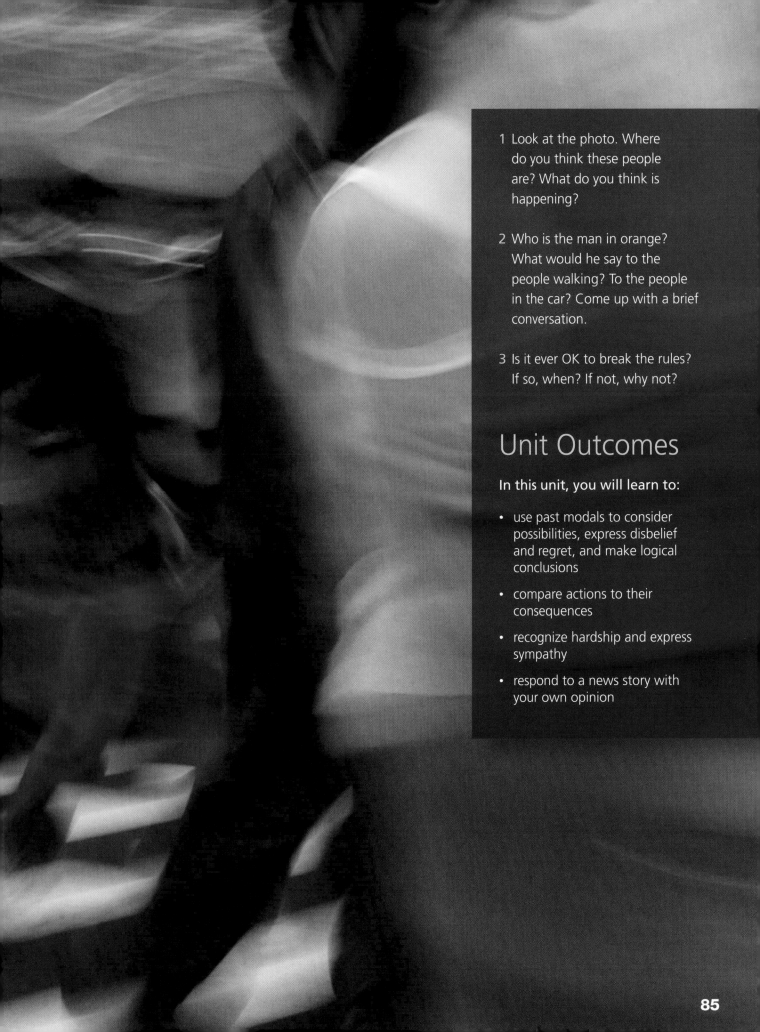

1 Look at the photo. Where do you think these people are? What do you think is happening?

2 Who is the man in orange? What would he say to the people walking? To the people in the car? Come up with a brief conversation.

3 Is it ever OK to break the rules? If so, when? If not, why not?

Unit Outcomes

In this unit, you will learn to:

- use past modals to consider possibilities, express disbelief and regret, and make logical conclusions

- compare actions to their consequences

- recognize hardship and express sympathy

- respond to a news story with your own opinion

Vocabulary

A Students often send text messages during class. Why do you think they do it? Discuss your answers with a partner.

---

consequences results or effects (of an action)

criticize to express disapproval by saying what's wrong with something

discipline self-control; an action taken to correct inappropriate behavior

disruptive causing trouble and stopping something from continuing as usual

get away with to do something wrong or risky and not suffer any consequences

get into trouble to be in a position where you will be punished for something

punish to take action against someone for inappropriate behavior

regulation an official rule (e.g., made by a government or school)

respectful to be polite and well-behaved towards someone (in authority)

restriction a limit on something

B Read these statements about texting in class. Who do you think said each one? Mark your answers and discuss with a partner. Which statements do you agree with? Why?

	Student	Teacher	Parent
1. I don't know of any restrictions on texting in class. It's not against the regulations, is it?			
2. I think there should be consequences for texting in class: for example, you should be punished in some way.			
3. It's a problem with discipline. Students who text in class are being disrespectful to their teachers and their classmates.			
4. All students would text during class if they weren't afraid of getting into trouble and being criticized by their classmates.			
5. Texting in class may be disruptive, but as long as they can get away with it some students will continue to do it.			

C Read the statements below. Answer the questions with a partner to discuss your opinions of these behaviors. Be prepared to share your thoughts with the class.

- talking in class without raising your hand
- looking at another student's work during a test
- coming to class without completing your homework

1. How are these behaviors disruptive? Which ones are serious discipline issues?
2. What are the consequences of these behaviors?
3. Which of these behaviors do people usually get away with?
4. What kinds of restrictions or regulations should be made to prevent these behaviors?

D In pairs, prepare a conversation where a student is caught texting in class by a very strict teacher. the teacher wants to punish him / her; the student asks for pardon. Use vocabulary from Exercise A.

Grammar

A Stella got in trouble for texting in class. Read the sentences in the chart to see what other students had to say about it. Then answer the questions.

Past Modals	
Use past modals with past participles to assess real or imaginary past actions.	
Disbelief / impossibility	Jen: Stella **couldn't have¹ been** texting. She lost her cell phone recently.
Possibility	Tom: She **might have² borrowed** a friend's phone to do it.
Logical conclusion	Amy: I heard she was texting her mother. It **must have been** something important.
Regret over an action that <u>wasn't</u> taken	Ed: Even so, she **should have waited** until after class to send a text.
Regret over an action that <u>was</u> taken	Min: I agree. She **shouldn't have disrupted** the class.
¹or *can't have*	²or *could have* or *may have*

1. Who is certain that Stella needed to send a text in class?

2. Who is certain that Stella was *not* texting in class?

3. Who thinks that Stella made a mistake?

4. Who thinks it is possible that Stella was texting in class?

B Choose the correct answer to complete each item.

1. She loves scary rides. She **could have / must have** been excited to go on the roller coaster.

2. He **shouldn't have / can't have** been in the meeting. He was sick at home that day.

3. I'm not sure where Mike is. He **might have / should have** gone to the store.

4. We just needed one more goal and we **could have / couldn't have** won.

5. Our team is better. We **may have / should have** won the game.

C What happened? Read about these five situations. On a separate piece of paper, write 2–3 sentences for each one. Use past modals. Then take turns reading your sentences aloud with a partner.

1. You arrived at your friend's soccer game. You see your friend on the ground being helped by another player. Everyone looks worried.

2. Your coworker gets a phone call and looks surprised. She picks up her car keys and runs out of the office. She leaves her purse behind.

3. You've arrived at school and it's time to submit your homework. When you look in your backpack, it isn't there.

4. Earlier this afternoon, you saw your friend's parents talking to your homeroom teacher. Later you find out your friend has been punished for a month.

5. This morning, you saw your neighbor sitting on the back of an ambulance with a bandage on his head. His car is damaged on one side.

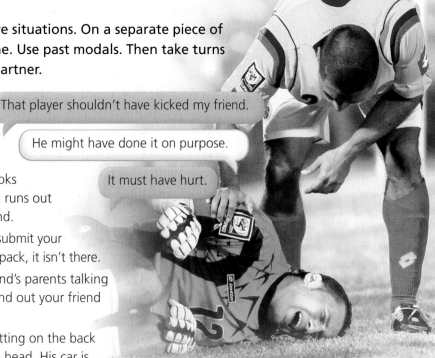

That player shouldn't have kicked my friend.

He might have done it on purpose.

It must have hurt.

Connections

A Read the information about a contest. What are the rules of the contest? Would you ever enter a contest like this? Why or why not? Discuss with a partner.

THE CONCERT OF A LIFETIME!
Register at www.freeticket.cengage and win a free ticket to the upcoming rock concert by the Regulation Nation.
Restrictions: Must be 18+. Limit one entry per person.

B Now read about Mary's situation. Then discuss the questions with a partner.

Recently I entered a contest to win a free ticket to a concert featuring my favorite band, Regulation Nation. The contest regulations were clear: only one entry per name. To increase my chances of winning, I also entered the name of my best friend, Paola, without telling her.

My friend's name was chosen and she won the ticket to the concert. I expected her to give me the ticket because I was the one who signed up for the contest and she knows the band is my favorite. I was shocked when my friend said she was going to sell the ticket at full price.

When I refused to buy the ticket, she sold it to someone else. I missed the concert and I criticized Paola for what she did. Now we're not speaking.

1. What did Mary do?   2. How did Paola respond?   3. What happened in the end?

C Read these statements. Indicate if you agree with each one. Then explain your answers to a partner.

	Agree	Disagree
1. Paola must have needed the money.	☐	☐
2. Mary shouldn't have broken the rules in the first place.	☐	☐
3. Mary couldn't have known that Paola would sell the ticket.	☐	☐
4. Mary shouldn't have criticized Paola.	☐	☐
5. Paola and Mary must not have been very good friends after all.	☐	☐
6. Mary should have just accepted the consequences.	☐	☐

D What should Mary and Paola do now? Come up with a solution with your partner and act out a conversation where they repair their friendship.

Listening

A You are going to hear a conversation about student Micah Green. Read this excerpt from the conversation. What do you think Micah did? Discuss in pairs.

Carly: Did you hear what happened? Micah got suspended from school. For five days!

Mark: You're kidding!

Carly: No, I'm not. He got in trouble for posting something online.

Mark: What exactly did he do?

B What happened to Micah? Listen and complete the story.

Micah Green went online to (1) _____ a teacher. He deleted the post a (2) _____ later, but it was too (3) _____. The school (4) _____ Micah by suspending him. The principal said that Micah's posting was disruptive to (5) _____ life. Micah is going to write a letter of (6) _____ to the teacher he criticized.

> **Listening Strategy**
>
> **Determining a Speaker's Attitude**
> Some set expressions can give clues to a speaker's attitude or feelings. **Sympathy:** *I'm so sorry to hear that. / That's too bad. / I can't imagine what she's / he's going through.* **Surprise:** *No way! / You're kidding!* **Agreement:** *I know! / Tell me about it!*

C Listen again. In your notebook, write key words to answer each question. Write "NM" if the answer isn't mentioned.

1. What does Micah think of Mr. Salazar?
2. What is Mark's opinion of Mr. Salazar?
3. How did Mr. Salazar react?
4. How did Ms. Stevens describe the incident?
5. How do Mark and Carly feel about Micah's situation?
6. What do Mark and Carly think about posting opinions online?

PRONUNCIATION Notice how Mark pronounces *should have* as *should've* in the sentence. *He should've kept it private.* For more information on reduction with past modals, see page 150.

Writing
Give Your Opinion on an Event

> **invasion of privacy** when your private life is disturbed in an unpleasant way
> **responsibility** something that is your job or duty to deal with

A Read the short article about student Micah Green. What did he do and how was he punished for it? Discuss with a partner.

> Student Micah Green was suspended from school for a week for criticizing one of his teachers online. Micah is the first student at the school to get into trouble for posting something on a social media site. Micah's parents will be meeting with the school's principal later this week.

B Read these online responses to Micah's situation. Which posting(s) do you agree with? Discuss with a partner.

soccermom
As the parent of a child who goes to school with Micah, I'm upset. This is an invasion of privacy. Micah was at home and using his own computer. He was not at school nor was he using school property. I don't know of any school regulations that say you can't express your opinions about a teacher on your own time. Are there any?

celticsfan
I go to Micah's school. As a student who spends a lot of time online myself, I can certainly sympathize with his situation. Does the punishment fit the behavior, though? Micah didn't use strong language and he took his post down after a short time. I think the school could have punished him in a different way—maybe by asking him to apologize to the teacher.

teacherman78
Being a teacher is hard work. We don't have very many behavior problems in my school, but there are some students who are disrespectful—just like Micah was. When an incident like this happens, you have to stop it right away. I think you need to make an example of the student. Was suspending Micah the right thing to do? I think so. Students need to take responsibility for their actions. What they do in and out of school has consequences.

C What do you think? Should Micah have been suspended? Write your own opinion to be posted online. Use the tips in the Writing Strategy.

D Exchange papers with another student. Read your partner's writing. Did your partner follow the tips in the Writing Strategy? Is your opinion similar to your partner's? How are your opinions different?

Writing Strategy

Effective Online Posts
When posting online . . .

1. Identify your role. *As the parent of a child . . . / I go to Micah's school.*
2. Explain how the issue relates to you. *As an Internet user myself . . . This is an invasion of privacy.*
3. Ask questions for further discussion. *Is that true? / Does the punishment fit the behavior?*
4. Try to summarize your ideas clearly or your audience may lose interest.
5. Remember to be respectful in your posting.

Video

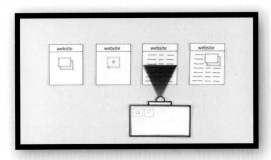 

A You're going to watch a video about how to protect your reputation online. Discuss the questions with a partner.

1. What kind of information is available about you on the Web?
2. How could someone harm your reputation online?

B Watch the video. Mark each statement true or false.

	True	False
1. Search engines take pictures of everything posted on the Internet.	☐	☐
2. You don't have to worry about a problematic photo if the image is deleted.	☐	☐
3. It's easy to control who sees the photos you put online.	☐	☐
4. It's possible to hide your postings from search engines.	☐	☐

C Read this list of do's and dont's for posting online. Try to guess the missing words. Then watch the video and check your answers.

Do . . .	Don't . . .
think of the _____ who will see the posting (grandfather, boss, etc.)	share everything _____
take _____ for images, videos, and stories you share	use people's _____
ask your _____ to think about what they _____ on the Web	
_____ before you click	
_____ the person who posted a bad photo of you and ask them to _____ it	

Ask

Answer Look back at your answers in Exercise **C**. Do you follow any of these suggestions already? In general, are you careful about protecting your reputation online?

Reading

> **anonymous** made or done by a person whose name is not known

A Look at the photos and the title of the reading. What do you think is the main point of the article? Choose your answer and discuss your choice with a partner.

  a. What we do in our private lives can show up online so there's a loss of privacy.
  b. There are new ways to uncover a person's identity online so it's impossible to hide.
  c. Anyone can post online so it's possible to get away with writing mean comments.
  d. Two videos online show that there are negative consequences to behaving disrespectfully in public.

B Read the article and check your answer in Exercise **A**. Were you correct?

C Find the words and expressions in the article that are the opposite of the ones listed below.

Paragraph 1

1. Opposite of *identified* or *known*: _____
2. Opposite of *leave alone*: _____
3. Opposite of *public:* _____

Paragraph 4

4. Opposite of *repaired:* _____
5. Opposite of *posted (a video):* _____

D Mark the statements that apply to the professional, the student, or both.

	The professional	The student
1. The person's behavior was caught on video.		
2. The video is online even now.		
3. The person damaged someone else's property.		
4. The person acted alone.		
5. The person knows that no laws were broken.		
6. The person said, "I'm sorry."		

E Summarize the professional's and student's stories using the chart in Exercise **D**. Then answer the questions with a partner.

  • What were the consequences of their actions?
  • Do you think video of them should have been posted online? Why or why not?

Ask

Answer Imagine that everything you said and did today was posted online. How would you feel? How might you change your behavior?

Nowhere TO Hide

1 We used to view the Internet as a place of freedom—a world all its own. When you went on the Web, you could be yourself, take on a new identity and pretend to be someone else, or simply remain anonymous. Whatever you said or did stayed online and did not interfere with your life offline. Likewise, your private life was your own, completely separate from your online identity. You didn't have to worry about things you said or did at work or school showing up[1] on your computer. You could act 10 goofy and it was no big deal.

Nowadays, new technology has changed everything, so that the separation between our two lives is no longer well-defined. What we do offline (in our "real" lives) can now be posted on the Web with a few easy clicks. With cheap cell phone cameras and free video hosting sites like YouTube readily available to anyone, photos and videos taken in public can be put online within minutes, sometimes with damaging results.

A professional in New York City discovered this the 20 hard way. She was filmed on a commuter train on her way home, arguing with the train's conductor. "I lost control," the woman said. "I was very tired from a long day at work and I said some things I wish I hadn't." That short argument had negative consequences because the scene was filmed by another passenger on the train and posted online that evening. Thousands 30 of people are still watching the video every month. "I was disrespectful, it's true," said the woman. "I didn't do anything illegal, but it feels like I did . . . because everyone is still criticizing me. It's been terrible."

A similar story happened in England when a young college student and his friends were filmed roughhousing[2] after a big football match. The young men damaged a car parked on the side of the road, and a video of the incident[3] was posted online and viewed by hundreds of thousands of people. "My friends and I 40 apologized to the owner of the car and offered to pay him for the damages," said the student. "We felt so bad. But the video didn't show that. It only showed us damaging the car." The video was removed after a couple days, but the damage had been done. "I almost got suspended from school over this. My parents punished me. This experience has practically ruined my reputation."

We know that we're losing our anonymity online. And now, it seems we are losing privacy and anonymity offline as well. There are no restrictions around recording 50 video of what happens in public and putting it on the Web. For now, you can get away with doing it.

It used to be a choice to go online and share yourself with the world. Now we are entering a time when someone else may be making that choice for us. In short, we may end up having a public face online—whether we like it or not.

[1] **showing up** appearing
[2] **roughhousing** fighting in a playful way
[3] **incident** an event

93

Speaking

surveillance the careful watching of
someone, especially by the police

A We are under surveillance in different ways in our lives.
Read about these situations in the boxes near each photo.
What do you think about them?

B Discuss the three practices shown on this page and the questions below
with a partner. Be prepared to share your opinions with the class.

- How do these different methods help us? How might they be an invasion
  of privacy?
- Which one do you think is most disruptive to our everyday life?
- What restrictions should be put on these different surveillance methods?
  - Are you sympathetic to people who get
    into trouble in any of these situations?
    Why or why not?
  - What should the punishment be if you
    get caught doing something illegal in
    each of these situations?

It makes sense for companies to monitor
their employees' computer usage.

I think it's an invasion of privacy.
Sometimes you need to take a break,
even at the office!

C Share your conclusions with
the class. Which practices
does your class support the
most? And the least?

In the UK, there are more CCTVs
(closed circuit televisions) per
person than anywhere else in the
world. They are used to track and
photograph your every move.

Large numbers of people pass
through airports every day.
To keep everyone safe, new
technology is being used to
scan passengers who may be
carrying dangerous items.

In one survey, the average person spent
one to two hours using the Internet for
personal reasons (e-mailing friends,
banking, shopping, etc.) while at work.
Companies are now able to monitor
exactly what their employees are doing
on their computers during the work day.

Expanding Your Fluency

A Look at these two pictures. Where are these people? What do you think might happen in each case? Discuss with a partner.

B Now read about the laws shown in the photos in Exercise **A**.

1. Where I live, your ticket is not checked when you get on the metro. Sometimes, however, police officers make spot checks to see if all passengers have a ticket. Last month, my friend got caught on the train without a ticket. She was so embarrassed. She has to pay a fine of 40 euros.

2. If you smoke, you have to put your cigarette butt in the trash. It's illegal to litter. Last week, my coworker was in a hurry. There was no trash can nearby, so he threw his cigarette on the ground. Then he heard a police officer calling after him. This is the second time he's been caught for littering in a year. He may have to pay a large fine. He's very upset.

C Create a role-play about one of the situations in which you or your partner pretends to know the person involved.

Student A: Tell Student B about your friend or coworker. Explain what happened and how you feel about the situation.

Student B: Listen to the story. Ask questions to get more details. Tell how you feel about it.

> My friend Hannah got in trouble on the metro.

> What did she do?

> She got on the train without a ticket.

> Really? She shouldn't have done that!

> I know, but she was in a hurry and . . .

Check What You Know

Rank how well you can perform these outcomes on a scale of 1–5 (5 being the best).

_____ use past modals to consider possibilities, express disbelief and regret, and make logical conclusions

_____ compare actions to their consequences

_____ recognize hardship and express sympathy

_____ respond to a news story with your own opinion

9 In the Wild

1 The animal in the photo is a macaque, or snow monkey, and is native to Japan. Is there an animal that is native to or often associated with your country?

2 In your opinion, can animals be intelligent? Which ones?

3 What story about animals was in the news recently? What happened?

Unit Outcomes

In this unit, you will learn to:

• use different forms of the passive voice

• use an outline to summarize ideas

• raise people's awareness about an issue

• write strong sentences to capture your readers' attention

Vocabulary

attack to try to hurt someone with physical violence

capture to catch a person or animal and confine it

cruel very mean or unkind

domesticated raised by people for agricultural purposes or living with people as household pets

endangered in danger of dying out completely

evolve to slowly change and develop over time into a different form

hunt to chase and kill an animal, usually for food

species a class of plants or animals that have the same characteristics

train to teach a person or animal how to do something

treat to behave in a certain way toward someone

wild free, untamed, not taken care of by people

> **Notice!**
> *in the wild* in nature

adv.	*treat (someone)* ***cruelly / fairly / poorly / well***
prep. + n.	*treat (someone)* ***with kindness / respect***
neg.	***mistreat*** to treat someone poorly

A Work with a partner to match an animal with a sentence. Then check your answers with the class.

Humans have been keeping animals as pets for thousands of years. How much do you know about three of the most common ones?

A parrot

	Dog	Parrot	Cat
1. This is the most common household pet in the world.	☐	☐	☐
2. This was the first wild animal that humans domesticated.	☐	☐	☐
3. Not only can this animal sing, it can also be trained to talk!	☐	☐	☐
4. Ancient Egyptians treated this animal like a god.	☐	☐	☐
5. Many wild species of this animal are endangered.	☐	☐	☐
6. This animal evolved from the wolf and was originally used for hunting.	☐	☐	☐
7. Some people believe capturing this animal and keeping it in a cage is cruel.	☐	☐	☐
8. If this animal wags (moves) its tail from side to side, watch out. It's warning you that it might attack!	☐	☐	☐

B Discuss the questions with a partner.

1. Do you, or does someone you know, have a pet? Is it trained to do anything?

2. What do you think of people who treat dogs like people (e.g., dressing them in clothes, feeding them at the table)?

3. Do you think it's cruel to hunt wild animals for sport? What about capturing and keeping them in zoos?

4. Name an endangered animal. Why is this animal at risk?

Grammar

A Complete the sentences in the chart with the passive form of sentences 2–6. Item 1 has been done as a model. Then check your answers with a partner.

1. People keep the animals in tiny cages.
2. Humans domesticated dogs 15,000 years ago.
3. Humans have trained them to do police and rescue work.
4. A volunteer is caring for the lost cat at the animal shelter.
5. The animal shelter will return the cat to its owner tomorrow.
6. Owners should keep their dogs on a leash.

Review of Passive Voice

simple present	The animals **are** *kept* in tiny cages. It's cruel.
simple past	Dogs _____ _____ 15,000 years ago.
present perfect	They _____ _____ **trained** to do police and rescue work.
present continuous past continuous	The lost cat **is / was** _____ **cared for** by a volunteer at the animal shelter.
simple future	The cat _____ **be** _____ to its owner tomorrow.
with modals	Parrots **can** *be taught* to communicate with humans. Dogs **should** _____ _____ on a leash.

❶ Forming the passive: Use a form of *be* + the past participle. With modals: modal + *be* + past participle
❷ To show who does the action, use *by* + noun: *The lost cat* **was found** *by a neighbor.* If it's clear who does the action, or if it's not important, don't use *by* + noun: *Parrots* **can be taught** *to speak.*
❸ You might use the passive if:
  • It's obvious who did something or the doer of the action is a general group of people: *Parrots can be taught to speak.* (We know humans are the ones teaching.)
  • The action is more important than who does it: *The boy was bitten by a spider.*

B Complete the sentences using the passive form of the verb provided in parentheses.

1. Every year, thousands of cats and dogs (simple present: *abandon*) *are abandoned* by their owners.
2. Recently a celebrity wearing a fur coat (simple past: *attack*) _____ by a group of animal activists. They say wearing fur is cruel. The celebrity says she (*should / allow*) _____ to wear whatever she wants.
3. In the last forty years, almost 20% of the Amazon rain forest (present perfect: *cut down*) _____ so that cattle (*can / raise*) _____ there. Scientists fear that another 20% of the forest (simple future: *destroy*) _____ by 2030.
4. A millionaire recently died, leaving all her money to her pet dog and nothing to her children. Now her wishes (present continuous: *challenge*) _____ by the family. They say it is unfair that a dog (simple present: *treat*) _____ better than a person.

C What should be done about the issues in Exercise **B**? Work with a partner to find at least one solution for each issue. Then share your ideas with another pair.

> Every year, thousands of cats and dogs are abandoned by their owners.

> I think the owners should be found and fined!

Listening

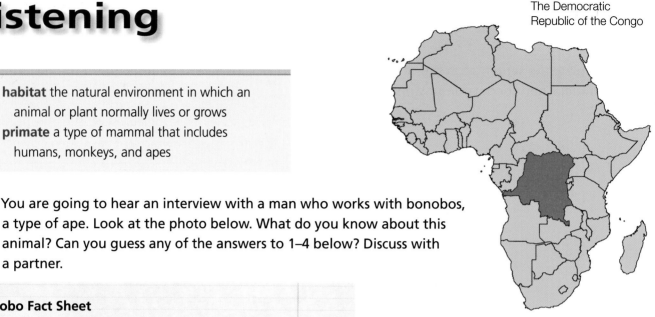

The Democratic Republic of the Congo

habitat the natural environment in which an animal or plant normally lives or grows

primate a type of mammal that includes humans, monkeys, and apes

A You are going to hear an interview with a man who works with bonobos, a type of ape. Look at the photo below. What do you know about this animal? Can you guess any of the answers to 1–4 below? Discuss with a partner.

Bonobo Fact Sheet

1. Country of origin in Africa: _____

2. How similar to humans: _____% of the same DNA

3. Behavior: _____

4. Endangered status: _____

   Reason: _____

Listening Strategy

Listening for probability
Listen for words and expressions like *possibly, probably, it's hard to say for sure, I think so, it hasn't been proven*. They are used to signal that a person is not 100% certain about something.

B Read the Listening Strategy. Then listen to the first part of the interview and do the following:

1. Complete items 1–4 above. Write only key words and numbers.

2. Then ask a partner: Which items are facts? Which are possible but haven't been proven? How do you know?

C Dr. Stern is going to describe a bonobo named Kanzi. Read the summary below. Then listen. Complete each blank with no more than three words.

Scientists are studying Kanzi because he's the first bonobo to learn to
(1) _____. The most surprising thing is that he wasn't
(2) _____ to use language. He learned it in the same way
(3) _____ do: he heard scientists talking to (4) _____.
Later, he tried to use words to (5) _____ with people. Today,
Kanzi can understand (6) _____ of spoken words and
communicates with people using a (7) _____. He also plays
(8) _____!

D Discuss the questions with a partner.

1. How is Kanzi special? If you could ask him a question, what would it be?

2. Do you think capturing and studying animals like Kanzi is useful or cruel? Explain.

Name: Kanzi
Species: Bonobo
Home: Great Ape Trust (in the United States)

Connections

Mammoths were a relative of the elephant that became extinct about four thousand years ago.

> **clone** a genetic copy of an animal that has been made in a lab using the DNA of another animal

A On your own, read the three situations. Come up with as many reasons *for* and *against* each situation as you can. List your ideas.

1. Ana is moving to another city and can't bring her dog with her. The pet needs a new home or it will be taken to an animal shelter. George has been thinking about getting a dog for some company and to encourage him to exercise more. However, he lives alone in a small apartment and tends to work long days, so the animal might be alone a lot. Should he take the dog?

2. Liz recently saw a movie that showed how animals are raised for food and she was shocked by how the animals were treated. Because of this, she's thinking about becoming a vegetarian. Should she?

3. Using cloning technology, scientists say that it is possible to bring back extinct animals, including those that died out recently (like some species of tiger) as well as those that became extinct thousands or millions of years ago (like mammoths or dinosaurs). Some of these animals would be kept in zoos; others would be released into the wild. Should scientists do it?

B Get into a group of four people. Follow the steps to discuss the situations in Exercise **A**.

1. Take ten small pieces of paper. Write "Yes" on five pieces and "No" on the other five. Shuffle the papers and place them face down.

2. Take nine small pieces of paper. Write the number 1 on three pieces. Do the same with the numbers 2 and 3. Shuffle the papers and place them face down next to the other pile.

3. One person starts. Turn over a paper from each pile.

   - 1, 2, or 3 is the situation you will speak about. *Yes* or *No* is the answer you will give to the question.
   - State your answer and give a reason to support it, using one of your *for* or *against* ideas from Exercise **A**. You cannot repeat a reason already given.
   - If your group members think you have given a good reason, you get a point. If you don't give a good reason or can't think of an answer, it's the next person's turn.
   - When you finish, return the papers to the bottom of each deck.

4. Play until everyone has answered as many questions as possible. Who has the most points?

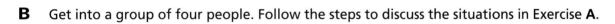

> No, he shouldn't take the dog. It's cruel for a pet to be left alone all day in a small apartment. No animal should be treated like that.

Reading

A Cover the Quick Stats to the right and try to answer the questions with a partner. Then check your answers.

1. How many years do elephants usually live?
2. How long do male elephants stay with their mothers? How about female elephants?
3. Are elephants endangered?

poacher a person who illegally catches and kills an animal

B Read the title of the article, look at the photos, and read the outline below.

1. What do you think the Wildlife Trust in Kenya does?
2. Read the article to check your answer. Then complete the outline with information from the reading.

The David Sheldrick Wildlife Trust in Kenya

WHAT IT DOES

The Wildlife Trust raises orphan baby elephants until they are _____ to the wild.
To date, it has returned over _____ elephants to the wild.

HISTORY

The Wildlife Trust was started in 19___ by _____.

HOW IT WORKS

Orphan babies arrive at the _____ in Nairobi.
Babies are cared for by _____ who stay with them _____ a day.
When elephants are _____ years old, they are _____.
Keepers reintroduce elephants to the _____ over _____.
Final goal: Elephants join _____.

THE BENEFITS

The work keeps elephant numbers from decreasing.
It maintains _____.

C What are some ways that humans and elephants are similar? Underline ideas that you find in the article. Did any of this information surprise you? Tell a partner.

D Using the outline, summarize for a partner what the David Sheldrick Wildlife Trust is doing in Kenya and why this work is important. In your opinion, what else can be done to help?

Orphan Elephants

Elephants, among the most intelligent creatures on Earth, may have no future without our help.

It's feeding time for the baby elephants at the David Sheldrick Wildlife Trust in Kenya. Here, orphan[1] elephants from all over the country are raised until they are strong enough to return to the wild. Most of them have lost their mothers and other family members to poachers or farmers protecting their land.

Moved[2] by the suffering of these animals, a woman named Daphne Sheldrick started a nursery[3] in Nairobi for orphan baby elephants in 1987. She named the project after her husband. Prior to this, she had cared for many of Kenya's native animals, but none interested—or challenged—her as much as the elephants. "Elephants are very human animals," says Sheldrick. "Their emotions are exactly the same as ours." In fact, studies now show that structures related to memory, self-awareness, and emotion in the elephant brain are very similar to those in humans. When young elephants arrive at the nursery, explains Sheldrick, "they've lost their families, and they come here filled with sadness and fear."

Enter the caregivers at the Nairobi nursery. With humans acting as their mothers, orphans are cared for by people called "keepers" who stay with them twenty-four hours a day. The other young elephants at the nursery help, too. Like humans, explains Sheldrick, "they are extremely social animals. Whenever we get a new baby here, the others will come around and lovingly put their trunks on its back to comfort it. They have such big hearts." When they are about 2, elephants are moved to a rehabilitation center in Tsavo National Park. Here, keepers slowly reintroduce the animals to the wild over several years, encouraging them to join one of the park's elephant families.

To date, Sheldrick's team has returned more than a hundred orphan elephants to the wild. The work being done not only helps to keep elephant numbers from decreasing; it has also helped to maintain the well-being of existing elephant populations. "The loss of older elephants," says one scientist, "and the extreme stress of seeing their family members killed, negatively influences a young elephant's normal development." When orphan females become adults, for example, they are less likely to care for the young properly. Male elephants become much more aggressive, which can also make them more of a danger to humans. When the young elephants are raised by stable[4] adults, however, these behaviors disappear.

Even after adult elephants have joined a new family in Tsavo National Park, some still come back to visit their human caretakers. In December 2008, Emily, a female that came to the Nairobi nursery in 1993, arrived at one of the rehabilitation centers one afternoon. "She'd given birth the day before, about a mile away," recalls one keeper. "She brought the baby here to show us her newborn." Even with a new life and family of her own, Emily—like other elephants—still remembered those at the Wildlife Trust who had loved and cared for her.

[1] **orphan** a child or animal whose parents are dead
[2] **moved** influenced emotionally
[3] **nursery** a place where the young are cared for
[4] **stable** calm, responsible

Video

VIDEO GLOSSARY

alert a warning, an alarm

anesthetic a drug that stops pain or causes you to fall asleep

collar (*noun*) an item that an animal wears around its neck; (*verb*) to capture an animal

GPS (global positioning system) a tool that allows you to locate or follow people or things on Earth

intercept to interrupt and stop something from happening

tag (*noun*) a device attached to someone or something that sounds an alarm; (*verb*) to put a tag on someone or something

A Work with a partner and do the following:

1. Explain what you already know about elephants. Why are so many of them being killed?

2. The title of the video is *Saving Elephants from Harm*. Watch the entire segment once through with the sound <u>off</u>. Then try to answer the questions.

   a. The people in the video are in Kenya. Who do you think they are?

   b. What exactly is being done to "help save elephants from harm"?

? Did you know?

Elephants live in a group called a *herd*. The female lead in an elephant herd is called a *matriarch*. Everyone in the herd follows her.

B Read the paragraph below and try to predict some of the answers based on what you've seen. Then watch segment 1 of the video with the sound <u>on</u> and complete the summary. Finally, use it to answer questions 2a and 2b in Exercise **A** again with your partner.

Iain Douglas-Hamilton and David Daballen locate and then follow a herd. Iain is in an (1) _____ and David is on the (2) _____. When they identify the female to be (3) _____, they shoot her. The anesthetic drug causes her to fall down. Once she's unconscious, the team has only (4) _____ minutes to attach the (5) _____. It will allow the elephant to (6) _____ with Douglas-Hamilton by sending an (7) _____ to a cell phone via text message.

C Watch segment 2 of the video. Then match an item (1–4) with an action (a–d).

How geo-fencing works

1. An elephant
2. The GPS in the collar
3. The server
4. A person

a. gets it and stops a herd before it reaches a human settlement.

b. sends an alert to a list of recipients.

c. crosses a virtual fence line.

d. sends a text message (SMS) to a server in Nairobi.

D Using the photo and your answers in Exercise **C**, explain to a partner how geo-fencing works. How does geo-fencing benefit the local people and help save elephants from harm?

Speaking

pesticides chemicals put on plants to kill insects

A Get into a group of three. Each person should choose one of the animals featured on this page. Then follow the steps.

1. **On your own**, read about your animal.
2. **Explain to your partners** in your own words the animal's current status and why people are concerned about this. Discuss what you think can be done about the problem.

Name: Siberian Tiger

Status: For years, tigers have been hunted for their fur and body parts (which are used in some cultures' traditional medicines). Their numbers have also been seriously reduced by the destruction of their forest habitat. Today, only 400–500 Siberian tigers—the world's largest cat—can be found in the wild.

Why the concern: Animal activists worry that the Siberian tiger may become extinct. In addition, because the tigers' habitat is being destroyed, it is harder for them to hunt. Though these tigers tend to avoid humans, they will attack and eat people if they can't find food.

Name: American Bumblebee

Status: According to a recent study, bumblebee numbers in the United States have dropped dramatically in the last twenty years. Some species have decreased by almost 96%. What's causing this? Climate change, pesticides, or something else—scientists aren't sure.

Why the concern: Domesticated bees are used to pollinate plants that give us many foods. Without the bees, less food will be produced, resulting in higher costs for consumers. Jobs are also at risk.

Name: Bottlenose Dolphin

Status: Though not listed as endangered, these animals are hunted worldwide for meat. Others are captured and sold for large amounts of money to aquariums around the world and used in animal shows.

Why the concern: Studies have shown that dolphins are not only playful, social animals, but that they are quite intelligent. Protesters argue that it is cruel to kill or cage an animal as smart as a dolphin.

B Imagine that you and your partners work for an international organization that will donate money to help one of the causes above. Which <u>one</u> would you give the money to? Why? Explain your reason to another group.

Writing

Create an Informational Brochure

A A student created the brochure below to raise awareness about koalas for World Animal Day. Read the brochure. Then discuss the questions with a partner.

1. What kind of headline did the writer use? (See the Writing Strategy on the next page.)
2. Describe the image. Why do you think it was chosen? Do you like it?
3. Does the background information explain clearly why this animal is in trouble?
4. Which fact makes the strongest argument for helping the koala?
5. Is the call to action written clearly? What is one more thing you could do to help?
6. Overall, do you like the brochure? How would you improve it?

Use **an attention-grabbing sentence** that uses one of the writing strategies.

Use **images** that grab your readers' attention.

Include **a call to action** that tells people what to do.

This little guy might lose his home. Won't you help?

BACKGROUND Though they can be seen in zoos all over the world, in the wild koalas can be found in only one place on Earth: the forests of Australia. For years, these unique animals were killed for sport and for their fur and almost became extinct. Fortunately, hunting koalas is now illegal. Protection programs have also introduced them into the wild again, which has helped their numbers to increase. Unfortunately, the koalas' natural habitat is still threatened as human populations expand into their forested land. Many koalas also die each year when they are hit by cars or are attacked by domesticated dogs that people keep as pets.

KOALA FACTS • Although it looks like a cute little bear, the koala is actually a kind of animal called a marsupial. Female marsupials carry their babies in a pouch on their stomach.

• For the koala, the tree is life. They live and sleep in trees, they eat tree leaves, and they get most of their water from the leaves they eat. If the Australian forests disappear, so will the koalas.

WHAT CAN YOU DO? Support or become a member of an organization like the World Wildlife Fund (WWF). Visit the site to learn more about how you can help.

B Work with a partner. You're going to create a brochure that raises people's awareness about an animal issue of your choice. Choose one of the animals in this unit or think of your own. Then design your brochure. Remember that it should have:

- an attention-grabbing headline.
- one or two compelling images.
- background information explaining what the issue is and two to four brief facts that will get people to care. You can use information you learned in this unit.
- a clear call to action that tells people what to do.

Getting a Reader's Attention When we write something—a brochure, a story, a news article—we want to get our readers interested in the subject matter immediately. One way to do this is to use an attention-grabbing headline or opening sentence. This might be . . .

- a question that makes you think: *Does having a pet make you healthier?*
- an interesting, surprising, or shocking fact: *In the last twenty years, 96% of these bees have vanished.*
- an emotional appeal: *Adopt a dog . . . save a life.*

C Exchange your brochure with another pair. Read their brochure and then answer questions 1–6 in Exercise **A** about it.

Expanding Your Fluency

| Monkey freed from zoo by keeper, still hunted by police | Drowning surfer rescued by dolphins happy to be alive | Critics and supporters battle as bullfighting banned in Barcelona |

A You are going to create a minute-long TV interview with a partner. Choose a news headline and, using it to help get you started, do the following:

Student A: You are the person from the news story (the zookeeper, the surfer, the critic or supporter of bullfighting). You're going to be interviewed by a TV news reporter about your experience. Work with your partner to invent a story. Think of answers to his / her questions that tell your story in a memorable way.

Student B: You're a TV news reporter. Think of five or six questions that you can ask your partner about his / her experience. If your interview is interesting enough, it will be shown around the world.

B Get together with another pair. Do your role-plays for each other. After you listen to the other pair's interview, answer the questions.

> You say that while you were surfing, you were rescued by dolphins. What happened exactly?

- Who was being interviewed? What happened?
- Did the person tell an interesting story? Do you think the story will be shown around the world?

Check What You Know

Rank how well you can perform these outcomes on a scale of 1–5 (5 being the best).

_____ use different forms of the passive voice

_____ use an outline to summarize ideas

_____ raise people's awareness about an issue

_____ write strong sentences to capture your readers' attention

C Change roles and repeat Exercises **A** and **B**.

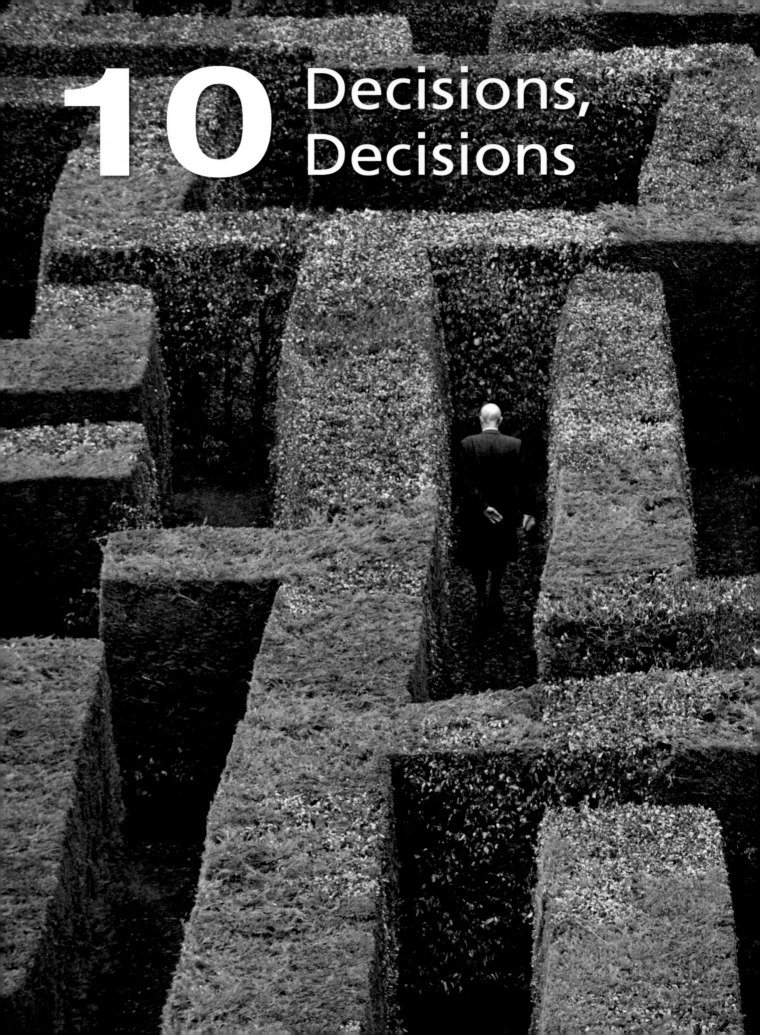

10 Decisions, Decisions

1 What does this image represent to you?

2 What was the last important decision you made? Did you make the right choice?

3 When you have to make a big decision, do you typically ask for help? If so, who do you ask and why? If not, why not?

Unit Outcomes

In this unit, you will learn to:

- use the conditional to make predictions and talk about hypothetical situations

- identify cause and effect relationships

- identify factors that influence decisions

- give reasons to justify a decision

Vocabulary

affect to influence or cause something to happen
change your mind to change your decision or opinion about something
concentrate to pay close attention to something
effect the result or change that one thing causes in a second thing
figure out to discover an answer or a solution to a problem

hesitate to not speak or act for a short time, usually because you are uncertain about something
process to review and consider information in order to understand it
rational logical, reasonable
react to respond or act in a certain way because of something that has happened
regret to feel very sorry about the outcome of something

A Look at the photos below. What are the people trying to do? Tell a partner.

B How much do you know about the brain and decision making? Complete each blank with a word from the word bank. Did any information surprise you? Tell a partner.

Word Partnership

Match each phrase with its definition:

keep (something) in mind	tell others honestly how you feel
make up your mind	remember
speak your mind	decide to do something

Did you know?

Your brain is able to (1) _____ large amounts of information at speeds of 200 miles (322 km) per hour! That's faster than a supercomputer.

When we have too many choices, it can be difficult to (2) _____ which *one* is best. In a situation like this, we often hesitate, change our mind many times, and then regret the choice we made!

A lack of sleep not only affects our ability to make (3) _____ decisions; it also makes it hard to concentrate and (4)_____ quickly. People who don't get enough sleep have a big (5) _____ on road safety, for example. Sleepy drivers cause over 100,000 car crashes a year!

C Complete the sentences with the words that describe you. Then explain your answers to a partner. Do you have anything in common?

1. When I have to make an important decision, I usually **react quickly and make a choice / take my time so I can make a rational decision / change my mind several times before I decide**.

2. I **often / sometimes / rarely** regret the decisions I make.

3. A lack of sleep **often / sometimes / rarely** affects my ability to concentrate in class.

Grammar

A Max is a college student who needs money for school. Read the advice he gets and then answer the questions with a partner.

Sam: You could get a part-time job in the evenings.

Max: Great idea. **If I do that, I'll have** enough money.

Jess: **If you had a scholarship, you would have** enough money.

Max: I know. I don't have a scholarship yet, but I'm planning on applying for one.

1. Look at the two **bolded** sentences. What does each describe: a possible future event or an imaginary situation? Write the sentences in the chart below.

2. What do you notice about the underlined verb forms?

The Conditional			
❶ With possible (real) future events		**❷ With imaginary (unreal) present situations**	
if *clause*	*result clause*	if *clause*	*result clause*

❶ This form of the conditional is used to make predictions and talk about possible future events. The verb in the *if* clause is in the <u>simple present</u>. In the result clause, the verb is in the <u>simple future</u>.

❷ This form of the conditional is used to talk about imaginary present events. The information in the *if* clause is not true right now. The result clause describes an imagined result.
The verb in the *if* clause is in the <u>simple past</u>. In the result clause, *would(n't)* + <u>verb</u> is used.
Note: *be* → *were* for all subjects in the *if* clause: If I / you / he <u>were</u> the teacher . . .

B Complete the sentences with the correct word(s). Then explain your answers to a partner.

1. If the teacher is sick tomorrow, we **won't / wouldn't** have class.

2. We'll go to the beach this weekend if the weather **is / will be** nice.

3. I'm broke, but if I **have / had** a lot of money, I **will / would** start my own business.

4. I **will / would** travel to the year 2100 if I **have / had** a time machine.

C Complete each item with your own ideas and discuss your answers with a partner.

1. If you _____, you'll probably get a good job.

2. You'll score high on the TOEFL if you _____.

3. If you drink too much coffee before bed, you _____.

4. If you miss more than a week of this class, _____.

5. If I were _____, I would(n't) _____.

6. I _____ more often if I had the time.

7. I'd be happier if _____.

Listening

A Listen to the conversations. After each, choose the best answer to the questions.

Conversation 1

1. The woman ____ a cooking class.
   a. regrets enrolling in
   b. wants to take
   c. has dropped

2. The man ____ the class.
   a. really enjoyed taking
   b. isn't familiar with
   c. has heard good things about

Conversation 2

3. Why does the man want to return the cell phone?
   a. There's something wrong with it.
   b. He's decided he doesn't want it.
   c. He's found a cheaper one somewhere else.

4. To get a full refund immediately, you must return the phone within ____ with ____ .
   a. three weeks; the original packaging
   b. a month; a receipt
   c. two weeks; a receipt

5. Will the man be able to get a full refund in the store?
   a. Yes
   b. No
   c. It's not clear from the conversation.

Conversation 3

6. The man and woman ____ .
   a. can't figure out when to meet
   b. are studying together from 4:30 to 6:30
   c. may or may not meet later today

7. When the woman suggests meeting at 4:30, the man hesitates because ____ .
   a. he's made other plans
   b. he has class
   c. he wants to invite someone else

B Read the sentences below. Then listen again, paying attention to each speaker's intonation. Choose the best answer for each one.

1. **Conversation 1** The woman says *I can't wait* because she **is / isn't** looking forward to her class.

2. **Conversation 2** The man says *Oh, that's great* at the end, because he's **pleased / annoyed**.

3. **Conversation 3** When the man says *Uh, yeah . . . maybe* he means **I'm not sure / Yes, I think so**.

4. **Conversation 3** The woman says *Oh, well . . . have fun* because she's **unhappy / happy** with the man's choice.

Ask

Answer

If you invited someone to do something (study together, see a movie) and the person said "maybe," would you expect the person to go with you?

Connections

hang out with the wrong crowd to spend time with bad people

A If a friend of yours started doing poorly in school, what would you do? Explain your choice to a partner.

   a. I'd ask what was going on and give some advice—even if he/she didn't want it. I always speak my mind.

   b. I'd talk to my friend, but I'd only give advice if I were asked for it.

   c. I'd probably wait for my friend to talk to me. His / Her problems are none of my business.

   Other: _____

B Read the situation below with a partner. Then choose roles and create a role-play. Perform your role-plays for another pair.

STUDENT A You and your twin sibling (brother or sister) attend a very well-known and expensive private school. You each receive a scholarship to go there, but must maintain good grades to keep it. Your twin used to be a really good student, but recently started hanging out with the wrong crowd and studying less. His / Her grades are beginning to suffer. You can't figure out what to do, but you're worried that if your sibling doesn't concentrate on school, he / she will lose the scholarship. You're also worried your parents will be angry with *you* for not helping your sibling.

   You want to find out what's wrong and persuade your twin to start doing better in school. Use the conditional to . . .

- make some predictions about what will happen if he/she doesn't make some changes.
- brainstorm some possible solutions to his/her problem.

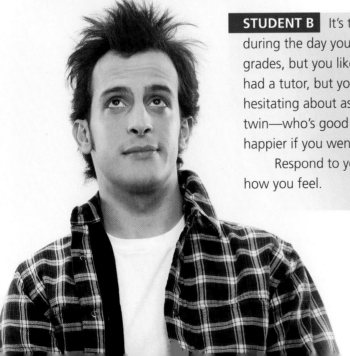

STUDENT B It's true: you're staying out late with your friends, and during the day you're having a hard time concentrating. It's affecting your grades, but you like hanging out with these people. It would help if you had a tutor, but you're not sure if your parents can afford one. You're also hesitating about asking for help because everyone compares you to your twin—who's good at everything. Sometimes you think maybe you'd be happier if you went to a different school.

   Respond to your sibling's predictions and suggestions and explain how you feel.

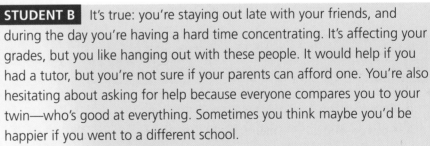

If you stopped hanging out with those people, maybe you'd do better in school.

Yeah, but I'd also never have any fun. I'm tired of studying all the time.

Reading

A Read the title and subtitle and look at the photo. What do you think this reading is going to be about? Tell a partner.

B Read the article. Then answer the questions with a partner.

1. According to paragraph 1, what happens to us during our teenage years?
2. In paragraphs 2 and 3, the author describes two factors that increase our tendency to take risks during our teen years. What are they?
3. Does the author think these two behaviors are mostly good or bad? Why?

> The prefrontal cortex—the part of the brain involved in making decisions, controlling our emotions, and planning for the future—isn't fully developed until we're 25.

C Choose the correct option for each item.

1. If something or someone is *maturing* (line 5), it is **developing / reducing**.
2. If you're *eager* (line 16) to do something, you really **hate / want** to do it.
3. Your *peer* (line 28) is someone who is **your own age / older than you**.
4. If you *impress* (line 43) someone, you cause the person to **dislike / admire** you.

> *ir-* = not
> What does *irrational* mean?

D Study the Reading Strategy. Then complete the cause / effect charts with information from the passage. Use no more than three words per blank.

Reading Strategy

Cause and Effect In the article, the writer examines the cause / effect relationship between the brain and behavior. A cause / effect essay answers these questions: Why does something happen? What is the result of that event? As you read, think about these questions to help you identify key details.

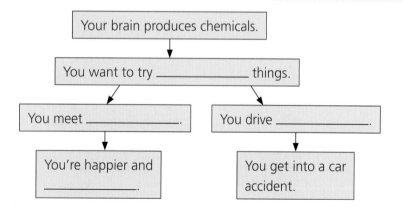

Your brain produces chemicals.

You want to try _____ things.

You meet _____.   You drive _____.

You're happier and _____.   You get into a car accident.

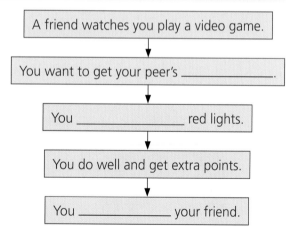

A friend watches you play a video game.

You want to get your peer's _____.

You _____ red lights.

You do well and get extra points.

You _____ your friend.

E Use the charts in Exercise **D** to answer the questions with a partner.

1. During our teen years, why are we so eager to experience new and exciting things? How can this benefit us? How can it be dangerous?
2. Peer approval is very important to us when we're teenagers. Why? How does the author use the video game to explain this?

Ask

Answer How important is peer approval to you? Do you care a lot about what others think?

The Teenage Brain

Why do teenagers act the way they do? Science may have the answers.

For years, scientists believed that human brain development was completed by the time we were 10 or 11. Recent studies, however, show that during our teenage years, our brain—especially the prefrontal cortex—is still maturing in important ways. When we're teenagers, our decision-making ability is developing and we're learning to make good choices. At the same time, we're more likely than ever to take risks. Is this normal? Scientists who study the brain say "yes." In fact, they believe that risk-taking and other "irrational" behaviors may actually help teens to become successful adults.

Take, for example, the teenager's love of thrills. We all like new and exciting things, but never as much as we do during our teenage years. During this time of our lives, say scientists, our brains produce chemicals that make us very eager to experience new things—the more exciting, the better. Although the need for excitement can lead to dangerous behaviors (like driving a car too fast and getting into a car accident), it can also generate positive ones. The desire to meet new people, for instance, can help us make friends, which usually makes us happier and more successful in life. Taking risks and trying new things can be challenging or even dangerous, but this behavior can also lead to useful experiences that will benefit us as adults.

Psychologist Lawrence Steinberg created a video game to explore an important factor that affects typical teenage behavior: the intense need for peer approval.[1] In the game, players try to drive across a town as quickly as possible. Along the way there are several traffic lights. Some lights turn from green to yellow as you approach them. You must make a decision: should you slow down and prepare to stop when you see the yellow light or speed up and try to go through the light before it turns red? If you get through the light before it turns red, you get extra points. If you fail, you lose time and points. When teens played the game alone, they took as many chances as adults. When a friend came into the room to watch, though, the teen almost always tried to go through more red lights. Their goal: to get more points and impress their friend. Adults who took part in the experiment, however, drove no differently with a friend watching.

Why did the teens react this way and try to impress their friends? We enter a world made by our parents, say scientists. But we will live most of our lives and succeed (or not) in a world run by our peers. Therefore, it is important that we are accepted—and respected—by that group, even if it means taking some risks to fit in.

Anthropologists[2] have found that almost all of the world's cultures recognize the teenage years as a time during which people seek excitement, take more risks, and struggle for peer approval. Doing these things can help us become successful, independent adults. But, say scientists, we must also learn that our actions can have serious consequences and find a balance between the two.

[1] **approval** support or praise; respect
[2] **anthropologists** scientists who study people, societies, and culture

Speaking

A Read the definition of **peer pressure**. Have you ever felt pressured to go along with the group even when you didn't want to? Tell a partner.

> If you do something because of **peer pressure**, you do it because other people in your social group are doing it.

B Read each situation and think about your answers to the questions.

1. You have a close friend that your other friends don't like. You're having a party at your house this weekend. If you invite your good friend, your other friends will be angry with you. If you don't and your close friend finds out, he/she will be hurt. What would you do if . . .
   a. you were in this situation?
   b. you knew your close friend wouldn't find out about the party?

2. You're assigned to work on a group project with three other people in your English class. You have to agree on a topic. One person suggests an idea and everyone else seems to like it. What would you do if . . .
   a. you had a better idea?
   b. you were new in the school and the most popular person in your class suggested the original idea?

3. Your cousin is a compulsive shopper: the minute he gets money, he spends it. Recently, he lost his job and he's asked you for a loan. You have the money but don't want to loan it to him. What would you do if . . .
   a. your other relatives started pressuring you to change your mind?
   b. you found out that your cousin just bought himself a new cell phone and laptop?

C Take turns asking and answering the questions in Exercise **B** with a partner. Explain your reasons for your answers. What factors most influenced your decisions? At the end, rate yourself and your partner on how affected by peer pressure you each are. Do your ratings match?

Peer Pressure Ratings

- **Approval addict** Peer pressure affects you a lot; your decisions tend to be strongly influenced by the group. You need their approval!

- **The in-and-out crowd** Sometimes you're influenced by others' opinions, but you also have a mind of your own and don't always give in to peer pressure.

- **Independent forever** You're not affected at all by peer pressure. You think for yourself and speak your mind, whatever the consequences might be.

D With your partner, come up with your own question about peer pressure (like the ones in Exercise **B**). It can be about friends, family, school, or work. Then exchange your question with another pair. Answer the question you get.

Video

appropriate the correct thing to do	**intuition** (*adj.* **intuitive**) a feeling that something
cognition a mental process used to think about things	is true even when you have no proof of it
inclination a feeling that makes you want to act in a	**plea** an emotional request
certain way	**rudimentary** simple, basic

A Read the information below and then ask a partner: Who is Tyler and what kind of research project is he participating in?

> At Princeton University in the United States, neuroscientists (people who study the brain) are doing research. They want to find answers to these questions: When we are faced with a dilemma (a difficult choice), how do we decide what to do? Which part(s) of the brain do we use to make our decision?
>
> Tyler, the research subject, is put into a machine called a *scanner*. Tyler will look at some pictures and he will be asked some questions. The scanner will record his brain activity.

B Watch segment 1 and answer the questions. Check your answers with a partner.

1. What decision does Tyler have to make? Summarize it in two or three sentences.
2. What do you think Tyler is going to do?
3. If you were in this situation, what would you do? Why?

C Watch segment 2. Then mark the correct answers.

1. **The majority / very few** of the people who participated in this study **would / would not** help the woman.
2. When we're faced with a dilemma, there's increased activity in which part(s) of the brain? Mark your answer(s) on the image.
3. The findings from this study suggest that we're more likely to help _____.
   a. an attractive person than an unattractive one
   b. a woman in danger than a man in danger
   c. someone nearby than someone far away

BRAIN MAP

EMOTION AND PERSONALITY
TOUCH
MOVEMENT
SPEECH
SIGHT
SMELL
BALANCE AND COORDINATION
MEMORY AND LEARNING
HEARING

- FRONTAL LOBE
- PARIETAL LOBE — CEREBRUM
- OCCIPITAL LOBE
- TEMPORAL LOBE
- CEREBELLUM
- BRAIN STEM

D Discuss the questions with a partner.

1. What does this study teach us about how we make decisions to help others?
2. Tyler's decision to help the woman was based on "an intuitive emotional response." How is using your intuition to make a decision different from using reason?
3. In what situations might you rely on your intuition to make a choice?
4. Do you think our intuition can help us make good decisions? Why or why not? Do you tend to rely more on your intuition, reason, or both when you make important choices? Why?

Writing
Showing Cause and Effect

A Read the scenario below and then one student's response to the question. What does he decide to do? What reasons does he give? Tell a partner.

You've been accepted to two universities. One is based in a small city near your hometown, where you're now living. Another is over 400 km away in a big city. Below is some information about the schools.

School near your hometown	School in the big city
• You'll live at home in your own room.	• You'll live in a dorm with two roommates.
• You'll be living in your hometown where everything is familiar.	• You'll be living in a big city that you've never been to before.
• All of your friends are going to this school, so you'll still see them all the time.	• You won't know anyone, so you'll make new friends.
• Classes will be small and you'll get lots of attention.	• Classes will be very large.
• Your school will be a local college where you'll get a good education.	• Your school will be a prestigious school where you'll get a good education.
• Tuition is affordable and you'll save money because you'll be living at home.	• Tuition is affordable, but doesn't cover other school-related expenses.
• Your parents prefer this college.	• Your teachers prefer this college.

Question: If you were in this situation, which school would you attend? Which factors would affect your decision the most?

Response: If I were in this situation, I'd probably go to the local school for two main reasons. First, it would be cheaper. When you go away to school, you typically eat in the dorm cafeteria, which costs extra. You also have a lot of living expenses that you don't have when you live at home. It can get expensive. If I went to a local school, I wouldn't have to pay to live in a dorm. I also wouldn't need to decorate my room. I'd save money on food, too, because I'd be eating my meals at home. **Consequently**, I'd be able to use my money for other things. Another reason I wouldn't move is that I would miss my friends and especially my family. I'm one of three children and we're all really close. If I moved, I'd only see my family during breaks. **As a result**, I'd probably be kind of lonely. If I went to the local school, though, I'd still see my friends and family all the time. **Because of this**, I'd probably be happier and do better in school. For these two reasons, I'd choose to go to the local school.

B Think about how you would answer the question in Exercise A. Then do the following:

1. On a separate piece of paper, list . . .
   - the school you'd go to.
   - two or three reasons for your choice.
   - what effects your choice would have.

2. Get together with a partner and explain your choice. Answer any questions your partner has and edit your notes.

C Using your notes, write a paragraph answering the question in Exercise **A**. As you write, remember to give two reasons for your choice. Also, explain what effects your choice would have. Use the information in the Writing Strategy to help you write about causes and effects.

D Exchange papers with a new partner. Does it follow the instructions in Exercise **C**?

> **Writing Strategy**
>
> **Showing Cause and Effect** Conditional statements show a cause / effect relationship. Words and phrases like *as a result, because of this, consequently*, and *so* also describe results.
>
> If I lived in the dorm, I'd probably eat out a lot. (Living in the dorm would cause me to eat out.) **As a result / Because of this / Consequently**, I'd spend a lot of money.

Expanding Your Fluency

A Get into a group of four. Come up with two "What if" questions together.

What would you do if <u>you could change one thing about yourself?</u>

B On your own: Take two small pieces of paper. On each, write a question and your reply **using the conditional (*if* clause in the past + *would*)**. Don't explain your answer, and don't write your name.

C Put your two slips of paper in the middle of the desk and mix them up with everyone else's answers. Then follow the steps.

1. One person should choose a paper from the pile. (If you get your own, choose another.) Read the question and the reply aloud. Try to guess who said it.

   - If your guess is *correct*, you get a point. You must ask the author one more question about his or her answer. Then remove the paper from the pile.

   - If your guess is *incorrect*, put the paper back in the pile.

2. Now it's another person's turn. Repeat step 1 until all of the questions have been answered. The winner is the person with the most points.

> ## Check What You Know
>
> Rank how well you can perform these outcomes on a scale of 1–5 (5 being the best).
>
> _____ use the conditional to make predictions and talk about hypothetical situations
>
> _____ identify cause and effect relationships
>
> _____ identify factors that influence decisions
>
> _____ give reasons to justify a decision

11 Rain or Shine

1 Look at the picture. What do you think the weather will be like in an hour?

2 Describe your perfect day. What's the weather like? What kind of weather is your least favorite?

3 Have there been any major storms in the news lately? Where? What happened exactly?

Unit Outcomes

In this unit, you will learn to:

- explain how weather affects your life

- make inferences based on information you have learned

- understand and use similes

- use phrasal verbs

Vocabulary

assess to judge or decide the quality or amount of something
consider to think about something carefully
cut off to disconnect
freezing very cold
frigid extremely cold
give up to part with; to let go of
intervene to become involved in a situation and try to change it

look after to keep someone healthy or safe
mild moderately warm
postpone to delay (an event)
recover to become well again
refuse to decline something
take off to depart
tolerate to accept something that you may not like

A Weather can impact our lives in many ways. What is one way it affects your daily life? Discuss with a partner.

B Look at the photos and captions. What do you think happened to Jerri Nielsen? What risks are involved in taking this type of job?

C Read Jerri Nielsen's story. Choose the correct verb to complete the sentences.

When Jerri was given an opportunity to work on the South Pole, she was so excited that she couldn't (1) **recover / refuse** the offer. She arrived in Antarctica ready for an adventure and she loved her new job. Halfway through her time on the South Pole, Jerri was shocked to discover she had cancer. At that point, Jerri (2) **assessed / postponed** her situation. It was too cold for a plane to come and rescue her. Any attempt would have to be (3) **assessed / postponed** until the weather became more (4) **mild / frigid**. Jerri's employers (5) **considered / looked after** sending a plane to rescue Jerri, but they canceled the plan because it was too dangerous. That was when the military (6) **cut off / intervened** in the situation because they had a plane that could fly in the (7) **freezing / cut off** air for a short period of time. A plane flew overhead without landing and dropped equipment and medicine for Jerri. She took the medicine to treat herself for several months. At the same time, she (8) **looked after / gave up** her colleagues as the doctor. And she waited. . . . Months later, she was rescued. Upon her return, Jerri received treatment and (9) **assessed / recovered** from her cancer. She wrote a book about her experience called *Ice Bound*.

Jerri Nielsen
Jerri Nielsen is a physician who gave up her job to work in Antarctica as the medical doctor for the Amundsen-Scott staff.

D With a partner, retell Jerri's story in your own words.

Ask
Answer Would you ever give up everything to move far away for a job? Would you be able to tolerate living in a place like the South Pole, cut off from everyone else?

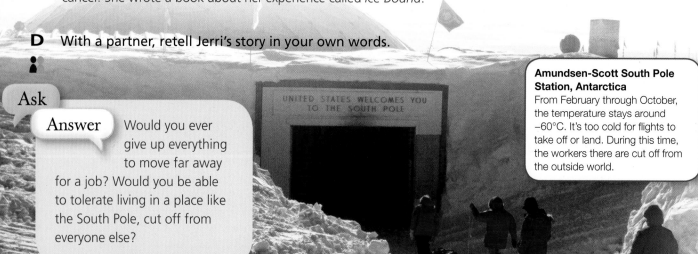

Amundsen-Scott South Pole Station, Antarctica
From February through October, the temperature stays around −60°C. It's too cold for flights to take off or land. During this time, the workers there are cut off from the outside world.

Grammar

Phrasal Verbs

A phrasal verb is a verb + preposition/particle. Some phrasal verbs are "separable;" the verb can be "separated" from the preposition/particle by an object (noun or a pronoun). Notice the placement of the pronoun in the separable verbs. Phrasal verbs have different meanings than the base verb on its own, as you will see in Activity **A**.

	With an object	Without an object
separable	She **gave up** her job. / She **gave** her job **up**. <s>She gave up it.</s> / She **gave** it **up**. Other examples: *put off, size up, think over*	She **bounced back** (recovered) from her illness. The plane **took off** on a dangerous mission. Other examples: *die down, pick up, step in*
inseparable	She **looked after** her colleagues. The doctor **looked after** them. Other examples: *find out, put up with*	

> Some phrasal verbs have three words. They are always inseparable: *How much longer do we have to* **put up with** *this rain?*
> *Every winter I* **come down with** *a cold.*

A Tam lives in Bangkok. Read his e-mails to his friend Pierre in Canada. Match each phrasal verb in the reading with a verb in this list that has the same meaning.

_____ assess   _____ discovered;   _____ postpone

_____ became less   learned   _____ recover

_____ consider   _____ increasing   _____ tolerate

_____ intervene

October 6 It took me forever to get to the airport, where I (1) **found out** my flight was canceled. The winds are (2) **picking up** and it looks like it's going to start raining again.

October 7 It rained all night. The winds (3) **died down** this morning, so I went out to (4) **size up** the situation. This is the worst flooding I have ever seen. I'll have to (5) **put off** my trip for a couple of days.

Bangkok floods of 2011

October 9 I haven't been able to write since Internet service has been cut off because of the storm. They're saying the military is planning to (6) **step in** to help people with the flooding. I can't (7) **put up with** drinking soda and eating noodles much longer. I wonder when Bangkok will be able to (8) **bounce back** from this storm.

October 10 I'm going to have to cancel my plans to visit you. Why don't you come and visit me in December? (9) **Think** it **over** and let me know your answer.

B Work with a partner. What do these weather expressions mean? Look up any you don't know. Then give an opinion or make predictions about these types of weather. Use phrasal verbs where you can.

torrential rain   a cold spell   scattered showers   pouring rain

boiling hot   a heat wave   snow flurries   heat stroke

> I can't put up with boiling hot temperatures. I prefer pouring rain!

Listening

A Look at the expressions below. What do you think they mean? Working with a partner, take a guess.

To describe weather	To describe people
break through	chill out
come down	freeze up
hold off	storm out

B Listen to the four conversations. Choose the answer that completes each sentence.

> **TIP** You might notice that many phrasal verbs have more than one meaning. *Pick up*, for example, can mean (1) *to increase* (without an object), (2) or *to lift* (with an object, as in *pick up a bag*), (3) *to physically obtain* (as in *pick up a newspaper from the store*), or (4) *to learn* (as in *picking up a new language*). Which meaning is used in Conversation 3?

Conversation 1

1. Jill went to a(n) ___ party.
   a. anniversary
   b. birthday
   c. retirement

2. There was a(n) ___ .
   a. argument
   b. performance
   c. announcement

Conversation 2

3. Bill is worried that ___ .
   a. people won't come
   b. he isn't prepared
   c. it will rain

4. Dan is ___ .
   a. confident
   b. unsure
   c. unhelpful

Conversation 3

5. Carrie wants to meet her friend at ___ .
   a. school
   b. Deena's house
   c. the theater

6. In the end, Carrie is ___ .
   a. staying home
   b. going out
   c. going to Deena's house

Conversation 4

7. Andy wants to ___ .
   a. be on the baseball team
   b. appear in the school play
   c. graduate early

8. Andy feels ___ about his chances.
   a. unclear
   b. negative
   c. positive

C Listen again. What do these words mean?

1. storm out (Conversation 1)
2. hold off (Conversation 2)
3. break through (Conversation 2)
4. come down (Conversation 3)
5. chill out (Conversation 3)
6. freeze up (Conversation 4)

> **Ask**
> **Answer** Have you ever stormed out of a room? If so, what made you so upset? What do you and your friends do to chill out? Think of a time when you froze up and didn't know what to do. What was the situation? How did it end?

Connections

> **break down** to stop working properly
> **call off** to cancel

A Look at the photos and answer the questions. Work with a partner. Where do you think these images are from? What do you know about the weather surrounding events like the ones you see here?

dust storm

blizzard

hurricane

B Work with a different partner. You are going to role-play a telephone call, sitting back to back so that you can't see each other's faces. Follow the steps. Use phrasal verbs in the box in your conversation when you can.

break down	*call off*	*chill out*	*come down*	*cut off*	*die down*
hold off	*put off*	*put up with*	*size up*	*be snowed in*	*take off*

Student A

Choose one of the photos above. You are on vacation in that place. Something has happened and now you have to cancel or change your plans. Imagine you are calling home to your friend, Student B. You should tell your partner:

What's happened

What you plan to do next

Student B

Your friend, Student A, is away on vacation (but you're not sure where). Suddenly the phone rings. It's your friend, calling you while still on vacation! You should ask your partner:

Where he/she is

How the vacation is going

C Switch roles and repeat Exercise **B** using a different photo.

> Student A: There's been a huge snowstorm.

> Student B: Is your flight going to take off as scheduled?

> Student A: I don't think so. The snow is really coming down.

> Student B: What are you going to do?

Video

batter to hit something with strong force
coastline the boundary between land and sea
defend to protect something against attack

erosion the gradual removal of rock and dirt
  by the weather (wind, the sea, etc.)
shrink to become smaller

A Look at the word bank and the photo. Answer the questions
with a partner.

1. What is the video going to be about?
2. What do you think is causing it to happen?

B Read these sentences from the video. What do the underlined
expressions mean?

1. If we didn't defend, nature would <u>take its course</u> and we'll lose more
land. *to take its course* = **develop naturally / change direction** and
come to an end

2. The sea walls themselves are <u>in a sorry state</u>. *in a sorry state* = in
good / poor condition

3. We simply can't continue <u>to paper over the cracks</u>. *to paper over
the cracks* = to fix something that is damaged so that it works
temporarily / permanently

C Watch the video. Complete the chart with key words.

1. The problem	3. What the government is doing

a. The _____ Sea is eroding the coastline.
    b. Great Britain is _____.
	a. The government is spending a lot of money to _____ the coastline.
	    b. Most of the money is used for _____ new sea walls and _____ older ones.

2. Why it's happening	4. What they're doing in Essex

a. The country is gradually tilting: Scotland _____ and England _____.
    b. Sea levels are rising due to global _____.
	a. They are flooding the salt marshes to _____ the coast.
	    b. They are not building more _____.

Ask

Answer   Do you know of other places in the world that are
slowly disappearing? Why is it happening?

salt marsh

Speaking

A Get into groups of four. Each student should read one story and then follow the steps.

1. Take turns explaining your story to the group.
2. What did you find surprising about each story? Discuss with your group.

❶ OTTO THE OCTOPUS

The staff of the Berlin Zoo look after many exotic animals, but none as popular as Otto the Octopus. He has a special skill. His handlers believe that Otto can predict when the sea is going to rise. When he floats at the top of the tank, it means that the seawater will soon be going up and the waves will be rough. If he sits at the bottom, the opposite effect will occur—winds will die down and the seas will be calm. The zoo staff recently postponed a boat trip to a nearby island due to Otto's prediction of "bad weather."

❷ THE DISAPPEARING CITY

The capital city of Mauritania (a country in West Africa) is known for its mild weather and central location within the country. It's also slowly disappearing . . . sections are being buried under sand from the nearby desert. After assessing the situation, residents tried building fences and pouring gasoline on the dunes, but nothing has seemed to work. At this point, they are used to putting up with the sand, but worried that they are losing their city.

❸ THE DAY IT RAINED FISH

On February 8, 2008, a strange rain started to come down in Kerala, India. As the winds picked up, local villagers reported that small, moving objects were falling out of the sky during the storm. It didn't take long to discover that they were fish! Scientists have some theories but are not sure how this could happen. The people who experienced it will never forget "the day it rained fish."

❹ MAKING IT RAIN

Have you ever considered what it would be like to change the weather? In the summer of 2010, scientists in Abu Dhabi did just that. They used a special machine to create more than fifty rainstorms—some with strong winds, hail, and lightning—on days when there were clear skies and no forecast of rain. They plan to keep on using this technology in areas where there is little to no rainfall. Needless to say, local residents were completely confused.

B These stories might all seem unbelievable, but only one of them is false. Which one do you think it is? Discuss with your group. Give reasons for your answer.

C Present your choice to the class and explain your reasoning. Your instructor will give you the correct answer. How many groups guessed correctly?

Reading

A Look at the photo of a tornado and answer the questions. Discuss with a partner. Then read the article to check your answers.

Tornado Alley, United States

1. What do you know about tornadoes?
2. Where and when do they occur most often?

B Read the article again. Cross out the one item from each list that doesn't belong. Then check your answers with a partner.

What the storm chasers measure	How long tornadoes can last	Where many tornadoes occur	Conditions necessary for tornadoes to occur
wind speed	a whole day	flat ground	warm wet air
humidity	an hour or more	crowded areas	cool dry air
temperature	a few seconds	good places for farming	winds from the north
time of day		central plains states	

C What do these numbers refer to in the reading? Write your answers on a separate piece of paper.

about 1,000	40%	48 kilometers (wide)	one in a thousand
one in five or six	F0 (winds of 64–116 kph)	F5 (winds starting at 419 kph)	

D Read these inferences that are based on information in the article. Then explain why you think the inference is true, based on what you read.

> **Reading Strategy**
>
> **Making Inferences** An inference is a conclusion that you draw about something you read. You can guess something is true based on the information you have—even when it isn't stated directly in the article.
> Statement: *The tornado caused more than light damage.*
> Inference: *On the Fujita scale, the tornado was greater than an F0.*
> (This is probably true because an F0 tornado only causes light damage.)

1. Inference: The storm chasers are driving in a rural area. (paragraphs 1 and 3)

   This is probably true because . . .
2. Inference: No one has ever filmed the inside of a tornado. (paragraph 2)
3. Inference: Tornadoes are not easily formed. (paragraph 5)
4. Inference: The path of a tornado is unpredictable. (paragraph 9)

Ask

Answer Tim Samaras has a dangerous job. What can you infer from the article about his personality? How similar are you to Tim? Would you ever do what he does? Why or why not?

STORM CHASERS

Two cars rush down a nearby dirt road straight at an approaching tornado. Storm chaser Tim Samaras, a 45-year-old electronics engineer from Denver, and his partner, Pat Porter, are in a van carrying equipment used to measure the tornado's wind speed and direction, air pressure, humidity (the amount of water in the air), and temperature.

Photographer Carsten Peter hangs halfway out the window of the other speeding car, which is driven by expert storm chaser Gene Rhoden. Carsten is excited. He wants to be the first person to film a tornado from the inside of the tornado itself.

The chasers can hear the tornado's jet engine roar and see it snapping power poles as they travel east past the local farms and directly into the path of the storm. It is not too far away, and the winds are picking up.

Tornadoes are among Earth's most violent natural acts. About a thousand of them happen in the United States each year, more than in any other country in the world. Some are weak and last only seconds, while others can cause damage for an hour or more.

Forty percent of all US tornadoes occur in the central plains states, agricultural[1] areas that are mostly flat. The "tornado season" occurs from March through July, when cool, dry air from the Rocky Mountains meets warm, wet air coming up from the Gulf of Mexico. In such open country you can see entire supercells (a rare kind of thunderstorm with especially strong winds), some as large as 48 kilometers wide. Only one in a thousand thunderstorms becomes a supercell, and only one in five or six supercells gives birth to a tornado.

Scientists measure tornadoes by the damage they cause. On the Fujita scale, named after Ted Fujita of the University of Chicago, an F0 storm does light damage with winds between 64 and 116 kph. The worst tornado, at level F5, does horrible damage with winds starting at 419 kph.

> "Storm chasers" are people who get close to violent storms in order to study and photograph them.

The clouds in the sky are spinning swiftly, and a confused bird flies in front of Gene Rhoden's car. And then a part of one cloud lowers and gathers into the shape of a funnel.[2] It spins like an angry ghost, no more than 3 kilometers from the storm chasers, looking like an alien[3] has come to Earth. The storm chasers are moving closer to the storm.

The tornado moves quickly through the fields, where it's destroying bushes and trees. Tim considers the situation carefully. He wants to find out all he can about the storm, but at the same time he must look after his team.

Before he can finish his assessment, the tornado does something strange. It seems to stand almost still, and then suddenly . . . it takes off, lifting up overhead. It's as if the sky were pulling a finger back into its fist. The winds have died down completely. The storm chasers pull their cars over to the side of the road to take a break. They've given up the chase for today.

[1] **agricultural** the science or practice of raising crops and animals (farming)
[2] **funnel** an object, which has a wide round opening at the top and a narrow tube at the bottom, used for pouring liquids
[3] **alien** a creature from another planet

Writing
A Vivid Description

A Discuss the questions with a partner.

1. How much does weather affect your daily life?
2. Why is there so much information (in newspapers, on TV, on the Internet) about the weather?

B Read Aleksei's essay about how a change in weather affected his daily life. What did you learn? Complete the first column about Aleksei's life in the chart below.

Where I live, we can have cold temperatures in the winter and gray skies with some snow. It doesn't typically get too cold, though, and it's usually sunny. That's why I was so surprised one week last February. We had a cold spell like no other. At one point, the temperature dropped down to –20ºC. No matter how many layers of clothing I wore, I couldn't get warm. It was so frigid that we had to turn off the water because otherwise the pipes would freeze and burst.

To get to school on time, I had to get up early because I couldn't depend on the bus. Usually I take a short bus ride to get to school, but during the cold weather the bus was often late, so I had to walk to school. When I arrived, I felt so cold, like an ice cube. That put me in a bad mood. It was too cold to be outside for very long, so I stayed home every day after school. I got a little frustrated and bored. My little sister is cute, but she was always bothering me. She can be as annoying as a puppy—always running around and making noise.

When the weather finally became more mild, I didn't have to wear as many layers of clothing so it felt as if I had lost 10 kilos. I hope we don't have another cold spell like that again!

	Aleksei	You
1. typical weather		
2. change in the weather		
3. impact on getting around		
4. impact on home life		
5. impact on mood		

C Read the Writing Strategy. Then look back at the reading on page 129; use the strategy to complete the sentences below.

Imagine you were with Tim Samaras, chasing a tornado.

1. The weather was crazy, like _____.
2. I felt as if _____.
3. The wind was as strong as _____.

> **Writing Strategy**
>
> **Using Similes** A simile is an expression that compares two things that the reader is familiar with in an unexpected way. We use similes (phrases with *like, as if*, and *as . . . as*) to make our writing more interesting and colorful for our readers.
>
> *When I arrived at school, I felt so cold,* **like an ice cube**.
>
> *She can be* **as annoying as a puppy**.
>
> *I didn't have to wear as many layers of clothing so it felt* **as if I had lost 10 kilos**.

D Now write about a time when the weather affected your life. First, complete the second column in the chart in Exercise **B** with your information. Then, write your paragraphs. Use Aleksei's essay as an example. Include two or three comparisons using "like," "as if," and "as . . . as."

E Exchange papers with another student. Read your partner's writing. Does it clearly explain how weather affected daily life? Does it use similes to create a vivid image?

Expanding Your Fluency

A Some phrasal verbs have more than one meaning. Read about these three situations. What does "break down" mean in each case? Match each usage to its definition below.

1. You are driving in the country with your friend when your car **breaks down**. There is a thunderstorm approaching and you realize you've left your cell phone at home and your friend's phone isn't getting any reception.	2. You're studying in London and it's been a long and cold winter. You have a friend who is originally from the Caribbean who isn't used to cold weather. You see your friend at school and ask, "How are you?" Your friend **breaks down** and starts crying.	3. You borrowed money from a friend to repair your car windows after a storm. You recently got paid at work and were supposed to pay your friend back but you **broke down** and bought a new surfboard instead. What will you say to your friend?

a. to give in to something; lose control

b. to stop working properly

c. to get upset; become emotional

B Work with a partner. Choose one of the situations and create a minute-long role-play about it. In your dialog, you must also use three or four phrasal verbs that you learned in this unit.

C Get together with another pair and do your role-plays for each other. At the end of the other pair's role-play answer this question: How did they resolve the problem?

Check What You Know

Rank how well you can perform these outcomes on a scale of 1–5 (5 being the best).

_____ explain how weather affects your life

_____ make inferences based on information you have learned

_____ understand and use similes

_____ use phrasal verbs

12 What's Your Game?

1 What is this a picture of? Have you ever done this sport?

2 What do you prefer: watching sports or playing them?

3 List as many sports, games, and activities as you can. Circle the ones that are competitive. Underline the ones you do with a team. Which do you prefer and why?

Unit Outcomes

In this unit, you will learn to:

- use reported speech to explain what someone else said

- evaluate the relationship between activities and personal qualities

- pace yourself as you write a timed essay

- use an outline to support a presentation or essay

Vocabulary

achieve to succeed in doing something after a lot of effort

beat to win against someone and defeat them in a competition

championship a competition to find the best player or team in a particular sport

coach a person who trains others to play a sport

commitment dedication to doing something

defend to protect from harm or injury

get used to to become accustomed to something

in shape fit, healthy

motivation a strong desire or willingness to do something

obsessed constantly thinking about something

opponent a rival, especially in a game

A Look at the photos below and tell a partner anything you know about these sports.

B Read what Derek and Ana have to say about rugby and kickboxing, respectively. Complete each profile with a word from the list.

Word Partnership

self- (combined with words in descriptions that relate to a person's own self). For example: *self-centered, self-conscious, self-defense, self-employed*. Find two more examples in Exercise **B**.

I'm a huge rugby fan. I grew up watching it with my dad and have been obsessed with the sport ever since. I played in university and now I'm the (1) _____ of a high school rugby team that has won several national championships. People ask me how we've managed to (2) _____ so many of our opponents. Part of it is talent and a team that works well together. But a big part is also each player's (3) _____ to training hard and giving his best *every* day. It takes a lot of motivation and self-discipline, but that's what wins a game.

A friend told me that she was taking a kickboxing class and convinced me to join her. At first, every session was an intense workout, and I'd be exhausted by the end. After several classes, I got used to the exercises and started doing really well. Not only have I learned to (4) _____ myself, now I'm (5) _____ too, which has really increased my self-confidence. Studying kickboxing has taught me that you can (6) _____ anything if you work hard enough.

C Discuss the questions with a partner.

1. How did Derek and Ana get interested in their sports? What are the benefits of each one?

2. Which personal qualities do these sports help people develop? Add ideas to make a list.

   • Commitment to hard work

   _____

   _____

   _____

3. How can these qualities help you succeed both on and off the playing field?

Grammar

Reported Speech

Use reported speech to explain what someone else has said. The verb tense, certain time words (such as *now, last week*), and pronouns can shift in reported speech.

Patterns in reported speech:
❶ verb + (*that*) clause: Ana **said (that) she was taking a kickboxing class.**
   use with verbs: *explain, insist, mention, say*
❷ verb + pronoun/noun + (*that*) clause: Derek **told me (that) he played rugby.**
   use with verbs: *convince, promise, remind, tell*
❸ verb + pronoun/noun + infinitive: Derek **encouraged his team to practice** more.
   use with verbs: *beg, convince, encourage, invite, remind, tell*

A Study the information in the chart. Then read sentences **a** and **b** below and do the following:

1. In sentence **b**, underline the pronouns and verbs that shift.
2. Which reported speech pattern (1, 2, or 3) does sentence **b** follow?
3. Use the verb *tell* and reported speech pattern 2 to report the sentences in **a**.

a. Direct speech: "I can't come tonight because I'm sick," said Al. "I think I ate some bad fish."

b. Reported speech: Al said he couldn't come tonight because he was sick. He thought he'd eaten some bad fish.

B Read the profile. With a partner, take turns reporting each statement about Marta's life.

When Marta was 14, a famous coach saw her playing soccer.

1. Coach → Marta's mother (*encourage*): "You should enroll Marta in a professional soccer camp."

   The coach encouraged Marta's mother to enroll Marta in a professional soccer camp.

2. Marta's mother (*explain*): "I don't have the money to do that."
3. Coach → Marta's mother (*promise*): "I'll take Marta to Rio and train her there."
4. Marta → her mother (*beg*): "Please let me go."

Marta's mother agreed. At 17, Marta was offered a spot on the Swedish women's soccer team Umea IK.

5. Coach → Marta (*convince*): "Take the job in Sweden."
6. Her opponents (*say*): "We've never seen anyone run that fast."

C Work with your class. One person says something about sports or games. The next person must repeat what that person said using reported speech and add something new. How long can you keep going?

I play chess.

Naomi said that she played chess. I've never played chess.

Naomi said that she played chess. Al said he'd never played chess. I like video games . . .

Marta Vieira da Silva
*Born in Brazil in 1986
*Soccer's greatest female player
*The female equivalent of soccer legends Pele and Ronaldo
*Is a Goodwill Ambassador for the UN

Listening

adjustment a change

handful a small amount of something

interpreter a person who translates what someone is saying into another language

NBA the professional basketball organization in North America

recruit to choose and try to persuade someone to work for your organization

A Professional athletes often play for teams in other countries. What challenges do you think they face when they move? Look at the profile of the basketball player below. What challenges do you think he might face? Discuss in pairs.

Name:	Jason Jennings (USA)
Age:	22
Years played a professional:	2
Country currently playing in:	China

B You're going to hear an interview with a professional basketball player. Listen and answer the questions below with key words and phrases. Then compare answers with a partner. Use reported speech to explain what the news announcers said.

1. Why is he famous?
2. Why is he in the news now?

> The news announcer said that Jennings was . . .

C What challenges has Jason struggled with? Listen and mark your answers.

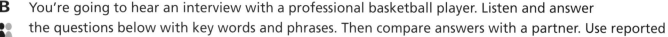

_____ 1. Difficult teammates and coaches

_____ 2. Missing familiar foods

_____ 3. Getting used to the weather

_____ 4. Making friends and socializing

_____ 5. Being the youngest on the team

_____ 6. A lack of privacy

D What did Jason say that made you choose your answers in Exercise **C**? Listen again and note the key phrases you hear on a piece of paper. Use reported speech to explain your answers to a partner.

Olympic Stadium, Beijing

> He said that it was hard . . .

E Discuss the questions with a partner.

1. In general, how do you think Jason feels about his first overseas experience playing basketball? What did Jason say during the interview that makes you think this?

2. What is Jason planning to do next? Do you think his experience with his next team will be different?

Connections

physical education (PE) a school subject in which students exercise or play sports

role model someone you admire and try to imitate

violence an act that hurts, injures, or kills people

A Answer the questions in the chart. Then interview three people and take notes on their answers.

What's the best way to get in shape? Why?			
Me	**Partner 1**	**Partner 2**	**Partner 3**

B Get together with a new partner. Report your findings in Exercise **A** using four of the following verbs: *say, tell, suggest, insist, explain*. Which response do you agree with?

> Carla explained that the best way to get in shape was to . . .

> **Notice!** *Suggest* can be followed by a <u>gerund</u> or a *that* clause:
> Carla suggested <u>doing</u> yoga to get in shape.
> Carla suggested <u>that the best way to get in shape was to do yoga</u>.

C With your partner, do the following:

1. Choose one of the interview questions about sports below or come up with your own.

   - Do athletes make good role models?
   - Is there too much violence in professional sports?
   - Do professional athletes make too much money?
   - Should kids be required to take PE in school?
   - Should a person leave school before graduating to pursue a professional sports career?
   - Is the popularity of video gaming a problem?
   - Your idea: _____

2. Using the question you chose, interview three people each. You and your partner should not interview the same people. On a separate piece of paper, take notes on what each person tells you. Remember to ask people to explain their answers.

3. Share your answers with your partner using three of these verbs: *say, tell, suggest, insist, explain*. Then evaluate all six responses. Which answer was the most common? Which was the most convincing?

D Summarize your findings. Then share them with another pair.

> We asked, "Do athletes make good role models? Most people said . . ., but one person had a different opinion. He suggested . . .

Reading

A You are going to read an article about a Chinese martial art called *kung fu*. Look at the photos and then tell a partner anything you know about it.

B What is the connection of the items below to kung fu? Scan paragraphs 1 and 2 and write your answers on a separate piece of paper. Then check your answers with a partner.

1. the Shaolin Temple in China *the birthplace of kung fu*
2. the fifth century
3. self-defense and battle

4. the city of Dengfeng
5. movie star, famous kickboxer, police or military officer

C Read paragraphs 3 and 4. As you read, think about the questions below. When you are done, answer the questions with a partner using your own words.

1. Who is Hu Zhengsheng? As a boy, why did he become interested in kung fu? How have his beliefs about it changed?
2. Think about the title of the article. According to Hu, what two sides are "battling for the soul of kung fu"? In his opinion, which one is winning?

D Choose the correct word(s) to complete each sentence.

1. *Adversity* (line 31) is a very **easy / difficult** situation.
2. A person with *character* (line 33) **is / isn't** able to deal effectively with difficult situations.
3. If you *get revenge* (line 37), you try to **understand / hurt** someone who has hurt you.
4. If a person *shows off* (line 51), he does things to **get attention / hide** from others.

E Read the statements. Circle T (for *true*) if you think Hu would agree and F (for *false*) if he would not agree. Underline the information in the article that helped you choose your answers. Then explain your answers to a partner.

1. A kung fu teacher's main goal is to show students how to fight well.   T   F
2. Kung fu films today are too violent and don't focus on the important things.   T   F
3. A kung fu master knows many different moves and why each is important.   T   F
4. The higher a student's kick or jump, the better at kung fu he or she is.   T   F
5. A lot of people today are studying kung fu for the wrong reasons.   T   F

Ask

Answer Master Yang told Hu that "pride defeats man." What did he mean by this? How can learning this lesson help one practice kung fu more successfully? How can this advice help a person in life?

A Battle[1] for the Soul[2] of Kung Fu

The Shaolin temple in China.

1 Every year, thousands of tourists from all over the world visit the Shaolin Temple in China to see the birthplace of kung fu. It is here, says one popular story, that in the fifth century, a teacher from India taught a series of exercises to the monks at the temple. The monks adapted these moves for self-defense and over the next fourteen centuries used them in numerous battles.

Today, the Shaolin Temple is just a few kilometers from the city of Dengfeng, China's modern-day kung fu
10 capital. In Dengfeng there are almost sixty martial arts academies with more than 50,000 students. These schools are attended by boys and girls from all over the country and every social class, ranging in age from 5 to their late 20s. Some arrive hoping to become movie stars or famous kickboxers. Others are motivated to learn skills that will get them good jobs in the military or police. A few are sent by their parents to learn discipline and hard work.

****

Hu Zhengsheng owns and runs a small school outside Dengfeng. At age 33, Hu has a handsome
20 face and projects a confidence won through years of physical and mental testing. Unlike the big kung fu academies, which focus on acrobatics[3] and kickboxing, Hu teaches his 200 students the traditional Shaolin kung fu forms that his teacher, Yang Guiwu, passed on

A Buddhist monk practices kung fu.

to him. Fighting is not the most important lesson of kung fu, Hu explains. He doesn't agree with how kung fu is often shown in the movies—a celebration of violence that ignores the more important teachings of respect for one's opponent. Instead, in his classes, Hu focuses
30 on respect and responsibility. In each of his students he looks for a willingness to welcome adversity—getting up before sunrise, practicing in the rain—using it to control themselves and build character.

From his own experience Hu knows that one's idea of kung fu can change as a person matures. When he was young, he was obsessed with kung fu films and dreamed of using the moves to get revenge on bullies[4] in his village. At age 11 he entered the Shaolin Temple and was later introduced to his teacher Yang Guiwu.
40 "When I met my master, I already had memorized many traditional moves," Hu says, "but he taught me the theory behind them—not just *how* to do something a certain way but *why*: He explained why I must move my arm a certain way. Why my weight must be on a certain part of my foot." Hu stands up to demonstrate. A strike[5] with your hand, he explains, is like a chess move. You hit the other person, but you are also prepared for how he will respond. Hu pauses. "Shaolin kung fu was not designed to entertain audiences or to attack schoolyard bullies."
50 There are no high kicks or jumps, he explains. A kung fu master doesn't show off. Pride[6] defeats man and makes him weak, teacher Yang had told Hu as a boy. "It is hard for me to convince my students of this, though," he sighs. Today everyone studies kung fu to achieve something. Hu worries that the real meaning of studying this martial art, to learn about oneself, is being lost.

[1] **battle** a violent fight
[2] **soul** the spirit or most important part of something
[3] **acrobatics** difficult physical acts such as jumping high and balancing
[4] **bully** someone who uses their strength or power to hurt or scare others
[5] **strike** a hard hit using your hand
[6] **pride** a feeling that you are better or more important than others

Video

> **ascent** a climb
> **ledge** a narrow stand outside a window where you can put things

A Alain Robert is often called "the French 'Spiderman'."
Look at the photos and watch the video once with the sound off. Then discuss the questions with a partner.

- What does Alain Robert do? How does he do it? Why do you think he does it?

B Read the statements. Then watch the video again with the *sound on* and mark the true statements. When you're done, correct the false ones so that they are true.

Alain Roberts climbing Tower One at Suntec City, Singapore.

Alain Robert . . .

	True	False
1. has climbed twenty buildings around the world.	☐	☐
2. normally uses no special equipment during a climb.	☐	☐
3. has never been arrested.	☐	☐
4. broke a world record.	☐	☐
5. has never rock climbed.	☐	☐
6. believes that climbing each building is a type of special test.	☐	☐

C Read sentences 1–4 below and think about what you've seen and heard in the video already. Then choose the synonym that could replace the underlined word in each sentence.

1. Would you <u>risk your life</u> for a sport?
   a. pay money   **b.** put yourself in danger   **c.** quit your job

2. As he climbs, one wrong move could be <u>fatal</u>.
   a. deadly   **b.** uncertain   **c.** difficult

3. Most people use <u>safety precautions</u>.
   a. insurance policies   **b.** special equipment to prevent accidents
   c. official permits

4. His goal is to <u>overcome</u> his fear.
   a. understand   **b.** ignore   **c.** beat

D Get together with a partner and explain . . .

- in detail who Alain Robert is, how he climbs, and why he does it. Use your own words.

- how you feel about Alain Robert. Do you admire him? Why or why not?

Writing
Explain Important Qualities

A Think about the people you learned about in this unit. What are the three most important qualities necessary to be good at kung fu? How about for an urban climber like Alain Robert? Select ideas from the list and then explain them to a partner.

commitment to hard work modesty responsibility strategy

courage   patience   self-confidence strength

determination   quick thinking self-discipline your idea: _____

B Read the short essay below by a student about her experience on a debate team. What does it take to be good at this activity? Complete the chart and then check your answers with a partner. You will complete a writing task on the next page.

What it takes to be a good debater		
What you have to do	**Reason**	**Qualities needed**
prepare by doing research	so you can debate the issue from all sides	commitment to hard work

The most important thing a good debater can do is prepare. Every debate focuses on a particular issue. In one debate I was in recently, we argued the pros and cons of playing video games. Whatever the issue, you must be ready to discuss it from your point of view and to respond to challenges from your opponents. Good debaters research the issue and study for hours before the debate so that they are ready. It's a lot of work and takes real commitment, but if you want to win you have to do it.

> Notice the words in bold. The writer uses these to introduce and transition from one idea to the next.

  A good debater should also be able to speak persuasively. In addition to researching the issue, you must also be able to present and defend your ideas confidently and in a convincing way. This will score points for your team. Getting used to doing this in front of an audience takes a lot of practice—and courage. Good debaters are constantly working to perfect this skill.

  Finally, a good debater stays focused even when things are difficult. During a debate, an opponent might say something unexpected or ask some hard questions. Some people get nervous when this happens, and this can cause a team to lose points. A good debater, though, stays calm and can think fast. Like speaking persuasively, this takes a lot of practice.

C Read the Writing Strategy. Then do the following:

1. Think of an activity that you enjoy now or played in the past. What do you have to do to be good at it? Why? Outline two or three ideas. Use the chart in Exercise **B** as a model.

2. Use your outline to write your short essay. You will have forty-five minutes to do this. Remember to save five minutes at the end to review your work.

> **Writing Strategy**
>
> **Pacing Yourself** On many standardized English exams, test takers are often asked to write a timed essay in which they must give an opinion. Assuming that you have twenty-five minutes total, remember to pace yourself and allow time for . . .
> • organizing and outlining your essay (about five minutes)
> • writing the essay (about thirty-five minutes)
> • checking your work (about five minutes)

> # Writing Checklist
>
> Does the essay . . .
>
> • identify the activity clearly?
> • explain what you have to do to be good at it?
> • identify which qualities are necessary?

D When time is up, exchange papers with a partner. Read your partner's writing and answer the questions in the Writing Checklist.

Speaking

A In the writing activity, you created an outline that described what you have to do to be good at an activity. You are going to use that outline to give a short (one- or two-minute) presentation. Do the following:

1. Read the Speaking Strategy.
2. Review your outline and, on your own, practice giving your presentation a few times.

> **Speaking Strategy**
>
> **Speaking from an Outline**
> **Getting Started: Preview the Topic** *I'm on the debate team at my school, and today I'd like to talk about what it takes to be a good debater.*
> **During the Presentation**
> Use transition words (like those in the essay on page 141) to help your audience follow you.
> Do not just read from your outline; remember to look up at your audience periodically.
> Try not to speak too fast, but be sure to pace yourself: you have two minutes total.
> **Closing: Summarize and Take Questions**
> *So, in conclusion, I think you have to do three important things to be a good debater. . . .*
> *Thanks for your attention. Any questions?*

B Get into a group of three or four people and do the following:

1. One person should give his or her presentation. It should last one or two minutes.
2. Those listening should take notes on a separate piece of paper using a chart like the one on page 141.
3. At the end of the person's presentation, those listening should review their notes and each person should ask the presenter one question.
4. Repeat steps 1–3 until everyone has presented.

> You mentioned that good debaters need practice learning to speak persuasively. What kind of practice do they do exactly?

Expanding Your Fluency

A Read the sayings below and then discuss the questions with a partner.

No pain, no gain.

You've got what it takes.

It's not whether you win or lose; it's how you play the game.

Practice makes perfect.

There's no *I* in *team*.

If at first you don't succeed, try, try again.

Run your own race.

1. What do you think each saying means?
2. Do you have a similar saying in your language? If so, what is it?
3. Do you agree with each saying? Why or why not?
4. Which of the sayings do you like the most and why?

B Choose one of the situations below. With a partner, create a two-minute role-play in which you use at least one of the expressions from Exercise **A**. Then do your role-play for another pair.

- You and a friend decided to take a yoga class together to get in shape. You thought the exercises would be easy, but after two weeks, you're still having a hard time getting used to them. You're feeling discouraged and are thinking about dropping the class.

- You applied for an internship with a video game company. You went on several interviews and everything went well, but the company chose someone else. You recently learned that a new position is available, but you're not sure whether to apply.

- You're working on a group project with two other people in your class. One of the people on the team is obsessed with perfection and insists on everything being done his/her way. It's driving you crazy and is making it hard for you to get motivated to do any work.

C Switch roles and repeat Exercise **B**, this time using a new scenario.

Check What You Know

Rate how well you can do the following tasks on a scale of 1–5 (5 being the best).

_____ use reported speech to explain what someone else said

_____ evaluate the relationship between activities and personal qualities

_____ pace yourself as you write a timed essay

_____ use an outline to support a presentation or essay

Pronunciation

Rising and Falling Intonation

🎧 **Intonation** describes the changes in pitch in spoken language. Generally, the pitch of a sentence or group of words rises or falls. The intonation tells you what kind of sentence you are hearing.

Below are the most common uses of **rising intonation**. Listen carefully to the pitch in each example. Note that it *rises* at the end of the sentence because the emphasis is on the information in the question.

- Yes–no questions with question word order:
  - May I have a glass of milk?
  - Will you help me with my chores?

- Yes–no questions with statement word order:
  - The movie starts at noon?
  - The bus station is on the corner?

Below are the most common uses of **falling intonation**. Listen carefully to the pitch in each example. Note that it *falls* at the end of the sentence. In a statement, this indicates that the sentence has ended. In *wh-* questions, the pitch is high at the beginning to emphasize the *wh-* word and falls at the end.

- Declarative statements:
  - The snow is gone.
  - The bowl is full.

- *Wh-* questions:
  - What was that noise?
  - When is the movie?

Practice

A Read and listen to each sentence. Decide if the intonation is rising or falling. Then write *rising* or 🎧 *falling* on the line.

1. You are still hungry after all that pizza? _____
2. Where are the car keys? _____
3. Do we have homework for English class tonight? _____
4. Everyone was late for dinner. _____
5. Do you think that painting is beautiful? _____
6. Are there any rooms left at the hotel? _____
7. The ball went over the fence. _____
8. Who was at the door? _____

B Write three sentences of your own with rising or falling intonation. Indicate which intonation your sentence has.

1. _____
   _____

2. _____
   _____

3. _____
   _____

Stress Changes with Prefixes and Suffixes

In English, adding prefixes and suffixes to words does not usually cause a change in stress. Here are some examples.

different	indifferent	differently
important	unimportant	importantly
arm	disarm	disarming

However, in some cases, adding a particular suffix will cause a shift in the syllable that is stressed.

| picture | picturesque |

Practice

A Listen to each word pair below. Mark the stressed syllable in each word to compare stress. The first one is done for you.

1. photograph   photographic
2. public   publicity
3. anticipate   anticipation
4. care   caring
5. correlate   correlation
6. rhetoric   rhetorical
7. cheer   cheerful
8. stable   stability
9. energy   energetic
10. play   playing
11. library   librarian
12. philosophy   philosophical
13. immediate   immediately
14. electric   electrician
15. hero   heroic
16. eager   eagerly

B Now, review the stressed syllables in each word pair. Which ones changed? Which ones did not? Write a rule about which suffixes cause a stress shift.

_____

_____

_____

Heteronyms and Stress Shift

 Words with the same spelling are called **homographs**. A subset of homographs are **heteronyms**: words that are spelled the same, but are a different part of speech and are often pronounced differently.

Word	Definition	Part of speech	Stress
project	A task or work that one plans to do	noun	PROject
project	To predict	verb	proJECT

You can often differentiate between heteronyms by identifying their part of speech. For most two-syllable heteronyms, the noun has the stress on the first syllable, while the verb has the stress on the second.

Word	Definition	Part of speech	Stress
digest	A collection of readings	noun	DIgest
digest	To take in or make use of, as in a meal	verb	diGEST
entrance	An opening through which to enter	noun	ENtrance
entrance	To fill with wonder	verb	enTRANCE

Note that you cannot apply this rule to all heteronyms. For example, the verb and noun *respect / respect* are pronounced the same. Also, some heteronyms have only one syllable, such as the noun and verb *row* (ROW) / *row* (ROH). Lastly, a few heteronyms, such as *invalid / invalid*, have more than two syllables.

Practice

A For each form of the heteronym, write the part of speech and show which syllable is stressed. The first one is done for you. Then listen to confirm your answers.

Heteronym pair	Part of speech	Stress
1. The police arrested the **suspect** late last night.	noun	SUSpect
2. I **suspect** that dinner is going to be late tonight.		
3. You will only **compound** the problem if you try to fix the sink yourself.		
4. The scientist invented a new **compound** that might help prevent allergies.		
5. We analyzed all the data from the latest **survey**.		
6. From the top of the mountain, I was able to **survey** the land for miles around.		
7. The lawyer did not **object** to the final ruling.		
8. The **object** in the sky last night was an airplane.		
9. My roommate will not **permit** me to use her computer.		
10. If we want to go fishing, we will need a **permit**.		
11. His **conduct** during the meeting was upsetting to everyone.		
12. Our director will **conduct** the orchestra during the festival.		

Linking Sounds

🎧 In spoken English, sounds in consecutive words are linked when the final consonant in one word is followed by an initial vowel in the next word.

- I've already made my bed.
- The dog tracked mud all over the kitchen.

They are also linked when the final consonant in one word is followed by the same initial consonant in the next word.

- His shirt tore when he did a flip.
- I made dinner last night.

Practice

A Predict where sounds are linked in each of the following sentences. Underline your predicted
🎧 linking sounds. Then listen to check your predictions. Circle the linking sounds to confirm
or correct your work.

1. There was music everywhere at the fair.
2. The bell rings at the end of each class.
3. Jamie said he was sorry for calling so late.
4. The sun rises each morning at 5:00 a.m.
5. Mary didn't have enough energy to finish raking the leaves.
6. Tina left the shower running this morning.
7. She thought the painting was outstanding.
8. When we got to the zoo, the lions were being fed.
9. My sister invited me to come, too.
10. Everyone thought the play was sort of funny.

Typical Stress Patterns in Three-Syllable Words

In English, many three-syllable words follow regular stress patterns. Listen to the pronunciation of these words, noting the rhythm of each pattern. (3 = the strongest stress; 1 = the weakest stress)

3-1-1 (stress on first syllable)	1-3-1 (stress on second syllable)	3-1-2 (stress on first syllable with minor stress on third syllable)
benefit	congested	simplify
terrible	inspection	manifest

Practice

A Listen to and then repeat aloud each three-syllable word. Then write the stress pattern you hear. You may want to mark the words as you listen and speak. The first one is done for you.

1.	magnify	3-1-2
2.	beloved	
3.	genuine	
4.	telephone	
5.	audience	
6.	penetrate	
7.	specify	
8.	bicycle	
9.	operate	
10.	manager	
11.	direction	
12.	excellent	
13.	triangle	
14.	fortunate	
15.	another	

Intonation Patterns and Relative Clauses

🎧 Many English sentences can be divided into chunks with internal intonation patterns. Some relative clauses provide additional, but not crucial, information about a <u>noun</u> or <u>noun phrase</u>. This type of clause is often signaled by the words *who*, *whom*, *whose*, or *which*. It is also separated from the main part of the sentence by commas to indicate a slight pause and has its own rising and falling intonation curve. In this case, the speaker mentions that the visiting sister is from Rio, but that detail is merely informative, not critical.

My sister,/ who lives in Rio,/ is coming to visit.

Other relative clauses provide important information about the noun or noun phrase. Without this information, the meaning of the sentence might be unclear. The intonation in this case does *not* fall after "My sister," but stays the same for the whole chunk, including the defining relative clause. In this case, the speaker must have more than one sister; the intonation and punctuation clarify which sister is visiting.

My sister who lives in Rio/ is coming to visit.

Listen to the difference between these two sentences.

- The shoes,/ which I bought yesterday,/ are the wrong color.
- The shoes that I bought yesterday/ are the wrong color.

Practice

A Read each sentence aloud. Which segments have their own intonation curves?
🎧 Separate each sentence into segments with a slash (/). Then listen to check your work. Revise your answers as necessary.

1. Barry taught the puppy that he adopted to sit.
   Carol taught the toddler, whom she babysits, several new words.
2. The rake, which I loaned to my neighbor, broke.
   The tool that I borrowed from my father is missing.
3. Susan's new dress, which is red, is very pretty.
   The new coat that Hannah bought is beautiful.
4. Marco, who doesn't care about clothes, wears whatever fits.
   The woman who just walked by wears the coolest styles.
5. That boutique, which just opened last month, has high prices.
   The mall that opened recently is close to my house.
6. Cats that love water are very rare.
   Cats, who don't like water, are no fun to bathe.

Reduction in Perfect Modals

 Reduction describes the process in spoken language when sounds are shortened and, often, changed slightly. Reduction occurs only in spoken language, not in formal writing (though you may sometimes see it written, for example, in dialogues).

Perfect modals in English include *must / should / would / could* + *have* + the past participle of a verb. When spoken, the *h* in *have* is usually dropped and the vowel sound is reduced to the schwa sound or *eh*.

- You <u>must have</u> left the gate unlocked; that is how the dog got out. ("mustehv," not "must have")

- We <u>should have</u> arrived earlier. ("shouldehv," not "should have")

- She <u>could have</u> gotten an A on the test if she had studied harder. ("couldehv," not "could have")

- If I had known you were going, I <u>would have</u> attended the party, too. ("wouldehv," not "would have")

 TIP In very informal spoken English, perfect modals are often reduced even further to: *musteh*, *woulddeh*, *coulddeh*, and *shoulddeh*.

Note that when *must have* is not followed by a past participle, it does not get reduced. For example: Bella said that she <u>must have</u> a new dress for the dance.

Practice

 A Say each sentence aloud, and then listen to the audio recording to check your pronunciation. Then say each sentence aloud again.

1. Jane would have gone to the movies with us, but she had to work.
2. I could have ordered pizza for lunch, but had a salad instead.
3. It must have snowed two feet last night!
4. I could have done my report on climate change, but someone else chose it first.
5. Juan thought he had his wallet with him, but he must have left it at home.
6. I'm so sorry; I should have remembered your birthday!
7. Pamela would have had ice cream, but there wasn't any.
8. I sent the package, but it must have been lost in the mail.
9. Danny did everything he could have done to win the contest.
10. Callie should have called Petra last night, but she came home too late.

Thought Groups

In spoken English, longer sentences can be divided into chunks, called **thought groups**. A thought group usually contains a major element, such as a prepositional phrase, a noun phrase, or a subject / verb. Also, it is signaled by a slight pause before and after it. Lastly, a thought group is just what its name implies: a phrase that coherently expresses a thought. Fluent speakers of English pace their speech to mark thought groups, which can in turn aid comprehension, add nuance, or emphasize or deemphasize certain details. Note: there is often more than one way to divide a sentence into thought groups.

Here are some examples of thought groups within longer sentences. The groups are separated by a slash (/).

- Scientists / are doing tests / to determine how humans decide / right from wrong.
- There are special areas / of the brain / that might control moral behavior.
- These areas / are associated with emotion / and what we call *social cognition.*

Practice

A Read each sentence aloud and separate the thought groups with a slash (/). Then listen to check your work. Revise your answers as necessary.

1. The sun was shining this morning, but then it started to rain.
2. Perry got up late and missed his train.
3. I hope to have my project done by the end of this week.
4. Everyone really enjoyed the movie yesterday.
5. By the end of the year, we should have finished redoing the spare bedroom.
6. The price of the washing machine was less than I remembered.
7. It was cold out, but I took the dog for a walk anyway.
8. The student won an award for her environmental work.
9. Susan sat by the phone, waiting to hear if she got the job.
10. Why didn't you come to the party last night?

Language Summary

Unit 1

adapt to change your ideas or behavior to suit a different situation **adaptation** (n.) **adaptive** (adj.)

ambitious needing exceptional effort and resources to be carried out successfully **ambitiously** (adv.) **ambition** (n.)

archaeologist a scientist who studies people and societies of the past **archaeology** (n.) **archaeological** (adj.)

average the normal amount or quality for a group of things or people **(to) average** (v., adj.)

buried under the ground and covered with earth **to bury** (v.) **burial** (n.)

come up with to suggest or think of an idea or plan

defeat to win a victory over someone in a battle or game **defeat** (n.)

determine to find out or to confirm certain information **determination** (n.) **indeterminate** (adj.)

generation the period of time (about 30 years) it takes for children to grow up and have their own families **generational** (adj.)

genetics the study of how certain characteristics (e.g., eye, hair, and skin color) are passed from one generation to the next by our genes **gene** (n.) **genetic** (adj.)

identical exactly the same **identically** (adv.)

invading entering a country by force with an army **invader** (n.) **invasion** (n.)

persuade to cause someone to do something by giving good reasons for doing it **persuasive** (adj.)

preserve to save or protect something for the future **preservation** (n.)

set out to start trying to do something

statistics numerical facts that are gathered through analyzing information **statistically** (adv.) **statistical** (adj.)

trait a particular characteristic a person has

typical showing the most usual characteristics of a person or thing **typically** (adv.)

Unit 2

accessible easy to reach or get into **(to) access** (v., n.) **accessibility** (n.)

adventurous willing to take risks and have new experiences **adventure** (n.)

atmosphere the character or feeling of a place **atmospheric** (adj.)

breathtaking very beautiful or amazing **breathless** (adj.)

charm the quality of being pleasant and attractive **to charm** (v.) **charming** (adj.)

convenience ease; suitability **convenient** (adj.) **inconvenient** (adj.)

destination the place you're going to (n)

diverse varied or different **diversity** (n.)

end up to arrive at a place or condition

get away to go away on vacation **getaway** (n.)

landmark well-known building or place

luxurious comfortable and expensive **luxury** (n.) **deluxe** (adj.)

outsider a stranger

particular someone difficult to please

perspective point of view

picturesque attractive, especially in an old-fashioned way **picture** (n.)

remote far away **remotely** (adv.)

rush to go rapidly **rush hour** (n.)

solitude the state of being or living alone **solo** (n.) **solitary** (adj.)

spontaneous coming from an impulse; unplanned **spontaneously** (adv.) **spontaneity** (n.)

spot place; location

timid someone who lacks confidence; shy

tranquil calm and peaceful **tranquility** (n.) **tranquilizer** (n.)

consume to use, especially in large amounts
consumer (n.) **consumption** (n.) **consumerism** (n.)

contribute to be one of the causes of something
contribution (n.) **contributor** (n.)

convert to change **conversion** (n.)

cut back on to reduce the amount of something
cutback (n.)

cut down to decrease

eliminate to remove something entirely **elimination** (n.)

entire the whole of something **entirely** (adv.)

generate to make or produce

give up to quit doing something; to renounce

impact a strong effect **to impact** (v.)

injustice a lack of fairness in a situation
justice (n.)

pollute to contaminate **pollution** (n.) **polluter** (n.)
unpolluted (adj.)

prevent to keep from happening **prevention** (n.)

produce to generate **producer** (n.) **production** (n.)

project to predict

reduce to make smaller in amount or number
reduction (n.)

rely on to depend on or use **reliable** (adj.)
unreliable (adj.)

residents the people who live in a certain place
(a house, neighborhood, city, country) **to reside** (v.)
residential (adj.)

reverse to cause something to move in the opposite
direction **reversal** (n.) **irreversible** (adj.)

roadblock a situation or condition that prevents
further progress; an obstacle

run out to use something (up) completely

source the origin or starting place of something

supply to give an amount; provide **supplier** (n.)
supplies (n.)

sustainable long-lasting or good for the
environment **to sustain** (v.) **sustainability** (n.)
unsustainable (adj.)

transmit send from one place to another place
transmission (n.)

appearance, to make an to come out in public **to
appear** (v.)

audience a group of people watching a performance
auditorium (n.)

audition a short performance given by a person to
demonstrate suitability for a show **to audition** (v.)

benefit a social event to raise funds for a person or
cause **to benefit** (v.) **benefactor** (n.)

charity an organization that helps people in need
charitable (adj.)

commercial related to the buying and selling of
goods and services **commercially** (adv.)
commerce (n.)

convince to persuade someone (to do something)

demo a brief recording illustrating the abilities of a
musician

emerge to come out and be recognized or noticed

encounter to meet **encounter** (n.)

enthusiasm a feeling of energetic interest in
something **enthusiast** (n.) **enthusiastic** (adj.)

fund-raising a way for schools and other organizations
to raise money for a particular purpose **to fund-
raise** (v.) **fund-raiser** (n.)

hardcore very committed (to something)

inspire encouraged (by) or motivated (by)
inspiration (n.) **inspirational** (adj.)

launch to start **launch** (n.)

logo a special design used by a company
or group

mainstream most typical or conventional

performance singing, dancing, or acting for an
audience **to perform** (v.) **performer** (n.)

promote to encourage the popularity or sales of
something **promoter** (n.) **promotional** (adj.)

realize to understand something, sometimes suddenly
realization (n.)

Language Summary

Unit 5

altitude height off the ground

catch (someone) off guard to be surprised by someone or something

client someone who pays a person or company for a service; a customer

collapse to fall down suddenly **collapse** (n.) **collapsible** (adj.)

disorientation confusion **disoriented** (adj.)

encourage to give someone confidence or hope **discourage** (v.)

freak out to lose control and behave in an extremely emotional or excited way

freeze to be unable to move or think

handle to deal with a problem or situation successfully **to mishandle** (v.)

injure to damage a part of a person's body **injury** (n.)

intense very great or extreme **intensely** (adv.) **intensity** (n.)

monitor to follow or check something regularly

ordeal a very difficult, stressful situation

panic to feel very anxious or afraid all of a sudden **panic** (n.) **panicky** (adj.)

rescue to save someone from a dangerous situation **rescuer** (n.)

risk taker an adventurous person, unafraid of taking chances **risk** (v.) **risky** (adv.) dangerous

rival a person you compete with **rivalry** (n.) **(to) rival** (v., adj.)

set off (for a place): to start a trip

soak in to look at or enjoy a place as much as you can

summit top

trapped unable to escape from a place or situation because something is stopping you **(to) trap** (v., n.)

Unit 6

adventurous willing to take risks and have new experiences **adventure** (n.)

affordable reasonably priced, inexpensive **to afford** (v.)

authentic real, genuine **authenticity** (n.)

bargain to talk with someone to try to get a lower price on something **bargain** (n.)

brand a type of product made by a particular company

browse to look around casually

check (something) out to look at

daring ready to take risks; adventurous **to dare** (v.)

deal something good you buy, usually for a low price

dependable reliable

discount a reduction in the usual price of something **(to) discount** (v., adj.)

fake not real **(to) fake** (v., n.)

fashion-conscious someone interested in the latest trends, whatever the cost **fashionista** (n.)

goods products you buy

imitator someone who copies what someone else does **to imitate** (v.) **imitation** (n.)

outgoing friendly and sociable

practical someone inclined toward useful and functional things **impractical** (adj.)

purchase to buy something **purchase** (n.)

quality how good or bad something is

recommend to suggest to someone that a thing or person would be good or useful **recommendation** (n.)

rip off something overpriced **to rip off** (v.)

self-confident someone who trusts in his / her own abilities **self-confidence** (n.)

serious someone who gives a lot of importance to things **seriously** (adv.) **seriousness** (n.)

sophisticated someone cultivated and elegant **sophistication** (n.)

(be) worth it to be expensive because its quality is good **worthless** (adj.) **worthy** (adj.)

Language Summary

Unit 7

availability the fact that something can be used or reached **available** (adj.) **unavailable** (adj.)

bottom line the total amount of money a company has made or lost over a time

commute the daily journey you make between your home and place of work or school **to commute** (v.) **commuter** (n.)

cramped not big enough for the number of people or things in it **to cramp** (v.)

delay when you have to wait longer than expected for something to happen **to delay** (v.)

fit in to feel that you belong to a particular group and are accepted by them **misfit** (n.)

get in arrive

keep in mind to remember something important (often given as a warning/advice)

option something you can choose from a group of alternatives **to opt** (v.) **optional** (adj.)

overwhelming difficult to fight against

perfect match two things that go successfully together

pull in/pull out arrive/depart (especially used for vehicles such as trains, trucks, and cars)

punctual on time; not late **punctuality** (n.)

reliable trusted to work or behave well **to rely on** (v.) **unreliable** (adj.)

rush hour the times of day when most people are traveling to and from work

tend likely to behave in a particular way **tendency** (n.)

transfer to go or move something from one place to another

Unit 8

anonymous made or done by a person whose name is not known **anonymously** (adv.) **anonymity** (n.)

big deal something important

consequences results or effects (of an action)

criticize to express disapproval by saying what's wrong with something **critic** (n.) **criticism** (n.)

damage to harm something

discipline self-control; an action taken to correct inappropriate behavior **to discipline** (v.)

disruptive causing trouble and stopping something from continuing as usual **to disrupt** (v.) **disruption** (n.)

get away with to do something wrong or risky and not suffer any consequences

get into trouble to be in a position where you will be punished for something

get suspended temporarily not allowed to go to school or class because you've done something wrong **suspension** (n.)

goofy silly or ridiculous

illegal not allowed by law **illegally** (adv.) **legal** (adj.)

incident an event

invasion of privacy when your private life is disturbed in an unpleasant way **to invade** (v.) **invader** (n.)

private only for one person or group; not for everyone **privately** (adv.) **privacy** (n.)

punish to take action against someone for inappropriate behavior **punishment** (n.)

regulation an official rule (e.g., made by a government or school) **to regulate** (v.)

remove (a video) to delete or eliminate; **removal** (n.)

reputation the opinion that people have about someone or something; how much they respect or admire it **reputable** (adj.)

respectful to be polite and well-behaved towards someone (in authority) **(to) respect** (v., n.) **(to) disrespect** (v., n.)

responsibility something that is your job or duty to deal with **responsibly** (adv.) **responsible** (adj.)

restriction a limit on something **to restrict** (v.)

show up to appear

surveillance the careful watching of someone, especially by the police

sympathetic showing that you understand and care about someone's suffering **sympathy** (n.)

Unit 9

alert a warning, an alarm **(to) alert** (v., adj.)

attack to try to hurt someone with physical violence **attack** (n.) **attacker** (n.)

capture to catch a person or animal and confine it **capture** (n.) **captive** (adj.)

clone a genetic copy of an animal that has been made in a lab, using the DNA of another animal **to clone** (v.)

collar an item that an animal wears around its neck **to collar** (v.)

cruel very mean or unkind **cruelly** (adv.) **cruelty** (n.)

domesticated raised by people for agricultural purposes or living with people as household pets **domestication** (n.) **domestic** (adj.)

endangered in danger of dying out completely **to endanger** (v.)

evolve to slowly change and develop over time into a different form **evolution** (n.) **evolutionary** (adj.)

hunt to chase and kill an animal, usually for food **hunt** (n.) **hunter** (n.)

intercept to interrupt and stop something from happening **interception** (n.)

pesticide chemicals put on plants to kill insects

species a class of plants or animals that have the same characteristics

tag a device attached to someone or something that sounds an alarm **to tag** (v.)

train to teach a person or animal how to do something **trainee** (n.) **trainer** (n.)

treat to behave in a certain way toward someone **to mistreat** (v.) **treatment** (n.)

wild free, untamed, not taken care of by people **wildly** (adv.) **wilderness** (n.)

Unit 10

affect to influence or cause something to happen

appropriate the right or correct thing to do **appropriately** (adv.) **inappropriate** (adj.)

change (your) mind to change your decision or opinion about something

concentrate to pay close attention to something **concentration** (n.)

eager to really want to do something **eagerness** (n.)

effect the result or change that one thing causes in a second thing **side effect** (n.)

figure out to discover a solution to a problem

hesitate to not speak or act for a short time, usually because you are uncertain about something **hesitation** (n.)

impress to make someone admire you **impression** (n.) **impressive** (adj.)

intuition a feeling that something is true even when you have no proof of it **intuitively** (adv.) **intuitive** (adj.)

keep (something) in mind to remember

make up your mind to decide to do something

mature to develop **to mature** (v.)

peer someone who is your own age

process to review and consider information in order to understand it

rational logical, reasonable **rationalize** (v.) **rationally** (adv.) **irrational** (adj.)

react to respond or act in a certain way because of something that has happened **reaction** (n.)

regret to feel very sorry about the outcome of something **regret** (n.) **regretful** (adj.) **regrettable** (adj.)

speak your mind tell others honestly how you feel

Unit 11

assess to judge or decide the quality or amount of something **assessment** (n.)

batter to hit something with strong force

below freezing below the temperature at which a liquid becomes solid **to freeze** (v.) **freezing point** (n.)

boiling hot very hot **(to) boil** (v., n.)

bounce back to recover

break down to stop working properly **breakdown** (n.)

break through to emerge **breakthrough** (n.)

call off to cancel

chill out to relax

coastline the boundary between land and sea **coast** (n.) **coastal** (adj.)

cold spell when the weather suddenly gets cold and stays cold for a while **cold** (adj.)

come down to fall to the ground

come down with to get sick with a particular illness

consider to think about something carefully **consideration** (n.)

cut off to disconnect **cutoff** (n., adj.)

defend to protect someone or something against attack **defense** (n.) **defenseless** (adj.)

die down to become less

erosion the gradual removal of rock and dirt by the weather (wind, the sea, etc.) **to erode** (v.)

find out to discover

freeze up to become stuck; unable to move

frigid extremely cold

frostbite a medical condition resulting from overexposure to freezing temperatures

give up to part with; to let go of

heat stroke a medical condition resulting from overexposure to high temperatures

heatwave a period of unusually hot weather

hold off to delay, not happen immediately

ice cap a permanent covering of ice

intervene to become involved in a situation and try to change it **intervention** (n.)

look after to keep someone healthy or safe

mild moderately warm

pick up to increase

postpone to delay (an event)

put off to postpone

put up with to tolerate

recover to become well again **recovery** (n.)

refuse to decline something **refusal** (n.)

scattered showers irregular rain over an area

shrink to become smaller **shrinkage** (n.)

size up to assess

snow flurries brief, light snowfalls

step in to intervene

storm out to leave a place noisily because you're angry

take off to depart **takeoff** (n.)

think over to consider

tolerate to accept something that you may not like **tolerance** (n.) **tolerable** (adj.)

turn down to refuse

Unit 12

achieve to succeed in doing something after a lot of effort **achievement** (n.)

adjustment a change **to adjust** (v.)

beat to defeat someone in a competition **unbeatable** (adj.)

championship a competition to find the best player or team in a particular sport **champion** (n.)

coach a person who trains others to play a sport **to coach** (v.)

commitment dedication to doing something **to commit** (v.)

defend to protect from harm or injury **defense** (n.)

get used to to become accustomed to something

handful a small amount of something

in shape fit, healthy **out of shape** (adj.)

interpreter a person who translates what someone is saying into another language **to interpret** (v.) **to misinterpret** (v.)

motivation a strong desire or willingness to do something **to motivate** (v.) **motivational** (adj.)

NBA (National Basketball Association) the professional basketball organization in North America

obsessed constantly thinking about something **obsession** (n.)

opponent your rival, especially in a game **to oppose** (v.) **opposition** (n.)

physical education (PE) a school subject in which students exercise and play sports

recruit to choose and try to persuade someone to work for your organization **recruiter** (n.) **recruitment** (n.)

role model someone you admire and try to imitate

violence behavior that hurts, injures, or kills people **violently** (adv.) **violent** (adj.)

Grammar Summary

Unit 1

Review of Past Tenses

simple past: Use for actions completed in the past at a specific time (sometimes inferred). Use time expressions like *a year ago, earlier today, last summer,* and *the other day*.	We **graduated** together. He **worked** there for a year.
past continuous: Use for ongoing past actions that may or may not be completed. Use with the simple past to describe what was going on when the action in the simple past occurred.	I **was working** all day yesterday. We **were studying** in college when we rented that apartment.
present perfect: Use for actions begun in the past and continuing up to now and for actions in the past that relate to the present. Use time expressions like *lately, recently, up to now, during the last two months,* and *this week*.	I**'ve worked** here for a year. **Have** you ever **studied** Portuguese?
present perfect continuous: Use to emphasize the length of an event. In spoken English the verb *to be* is almost always a contraction.	Recently, I**'ve been working** too much. She**'s been waiting** for an hour!

- Use *for* (+ a <u>period</u> of time) and *since* (+ a <u>specific point</u> in time) with the perfect tenses to describe "time up to now." Use *for* (but not *since*) with the simple past tense for a time period that has come to an end.

Unit 2

Uses of Infinitives and Gerunds

1. purpose infinitive	*Last summer I went overseas* **to study** *English.*
2. *it + be +* adjective *+* infinitive	*It was great* **to experience** *life in a small town.*
3. *too +* adjective *+* infinitive	*At first, it was too hard* **to communicate** *in English.*
4. gerunds as subjects	***Learning*** *the language was essential.*
5. adjective + preposition + gerund	*The small town is famous for* **skiing** *in the winter and* **hiking** *in the summer.*
6. verb + preposition + gerund	*I look forward to* **going back** *next year!*

Unit 3

Review of Future Forms

definite plans	**I'm going to take** the TOEFL next Saturday. **I'm taking** the TOEFL next Saturday.
predictions	By 2040, there **are going to be** over 8 billion people on Earth. By 2040, there **will be** over 8 billion people on Earth.
promises	**I'll call** you tonight after I get home. I **won't** forget.
ongoing future actions	Within ten years, Germany **will be using** less oil and more renewable sources.

Unit 4

- Note that the chart below is list of common patterns and tendencies. You may hear or see other uses, but learning these patterns will allow you to use infinitive complements in English correctly and naturally.

Infinitive Complements

Infinitive complements that follow the pattern **verb + object + infinitive** fall into some common verb groups including ❶ *persuade* verbs (*advise, cause, convince*), ❷ *want* verbs (*expect, need*), ❸ *believe* verbs (*consider, recognize*), and ❹ *plan* verbs (*arrange*). Group ❺ verbs are *have, let,* and *make*.

❶ Verb + object + infinitive	She **advised** me to take the job.
❷ Verb + (object) + infinitive	She **expects** me to apply. I **need** to find a job.
❸ Verb + object + infinitive of *be*	We **consider** him to be the best singer.
❹ Verb + *for* + object + infinitive	They **arranged** for me to have an interview.
❺ Verb + object + base form	His music **makes** me feel happy.

Group ❶: the object is required.   Group ❷: the object is optional.
Group ❸: follows the pattern **verb + object + infinitive**, and the infinitive is usually *to be*.
Group ❹: follows the pattern **verb + *for* + object + infinitive**.
Group ❺: follows the same basic pattern, but requires the base form of the verb rather than the full infinitive.

- Note that the presence or absence of the object defines the meaning of the sentence.

    She expects for me to apply. (She thinks I will apply.)
    She expects to apply. (She is planning to apply herself.)

Unit 5

Adverbial Clauses

Adverbial clauses explain when, why, where, or in what way something happened. Adverbial clauses begin with a *connecting word*. When the clause starts a sentence, it is followed by a comma.

Time: *after, since, whenever, as soon as, until, while, before, when*	**After the mine collapsed**, the men were trapped. The men were trapped **after the mine collapsed**.
Reason: *because, since*	**Because the mine collapsed**, the men were trapped.
Contrast: *although, (even) though*	**Even though it was hard**, they survived for weeks.
Purpose: *so (that)*	They closed the mine **so (that) an accident doesn't happen again**.
Before, after, during, since, and *until* can also be followed by a <u>noun phrase</u>.	**Before** <u>the collapse</u>, the men heard a sound. **During** <u>the collapse</u>, one man was injured.

Adjective Clauses with Subject Relative Pronouns

who = for people	❶ People **who visit Dubai during the shopping festival** can get some great deals.
which = for things	❷ The festival, **which gets over three million visitors**, lasts several weeks.
that = for people and things	❸ Nadia is someone **that spends a lot on clothes**. ❹ It's a festival **that takes place every year**.
subject-verb agreement	❺ It's a <u>shop</u> **that <u>sells</u> discount electronics**. ❻ They're <u>shops</u> **that <u>sell</u> designer handbags**.

Adjective clauses give more information about a noun and begin with a relative pronoun (*who, which, that*).
In ❶, the adjective clause gives <u>necessary information</u> about the subject. It completes the meaning of the sentence.
In ❷, the adjective clause gives <u>extra information</u> about the subject. You don't need it to complete the meaning of the sentence. It is separated from the main clause by commas.

- When an adjective clause gives extra information, *that* cannot be used:
    The festival, ~~that~~ which gets over three million visitors . . .

- Don't repeat the subject after the relative pronoun:
    He's a person who ~~he~~ spends a lot on clothes.

- In everyday spoken English, *that* is used much more often than *which* to describe things.
    Did you buy the jacket **that** was on sale?

Unit 7

Comparative Forms

	more than . . .	less than . . .	equal to . . .
Adjectives	Taking a taxi is **faster** and **more reliable than** taking the subway.	The subways are **less reliable than** they used to be. They are **not as nice as** they once were.	During rush hour, walking is **as fast as** taking the bus.
Adverbs	The trains run **faster** and **more frequently** than the bus.	The trains run **less frequently** on weekends than they do on weekdays.	The old trains run **as smoothly as** the new ones.
Noncount nouns	After I quit, I had **more time than** I used to.	As a new parent, I have **less time than** I used to.	I spend **as much** time working **as** (I did) before.
Count nouns	The local train makes **more stops than** the express (does).	The express train makes **fewer stops than** the local (does).	The Blue Line has **as many riders** as it did last year.
Irregular forms: good → better, bad → worse, far → further			

- We don't usually use *less* with one-syllable adjectives. We use *not as . . . as* instead.
    ~~The bus is less fast than the train~~.
    The bus is not as fast as the train.

- Here is an additional summary of comparative forms for review.

Single-syllable adjectives add –er (or just). If the adjective ends in a single vowel and a consonant, double the final consonant.	clean → cleaner cute → cuter big → bigger
Two-syllable adjectives ending in –y, -le, and –ly usually take –er.	funny → funnier simple → simpler careful → careful
Some adjectives can have two comparative forms.	friendly → friendlier / more friendly happy → happier / more happy handsome → handsomer / more handsome
Other adjectives with two syllables and adjectives with more than two syllables usually take more.	complex → more complex intelligent → more intelligent beautiful → more beautiful
Adverbs ending in –ly usually take more.	softly → more softly quickly → more quickly regularly → more regularly

Unit 8

Past Modals	
Use past modals with past participles to assess real or imaginary past actions.	
Disbelief / impossibility	Jen: Stella **couldn't have**[1] **been** texting. She lost her cell phone recently.
Possibility	Tom: She **might have**[2] **borrowed** a friend's phone to do it.
Logical conclusion	Amy: I heard she was texting her mother. It **must have been** something important.
Regret over an action that <u>wasn't</u> taken	Ed: Even so, she **should have waited** until after class to send a text.
Regret over an action that <u>was</u> taken	Mina: I agree. She **shouldn't have disrupted** the class.
[1]or can't have	[2]or could have or may have

- Note that while *mustn't have* is used in the context of a logical conclusion, the present/future *mustn't* is used to prohibit someone from doing something.

    You mustn't have parked on this street—I don't see you car anywhere. (logical conclusion)

    You mustn't park here because of street cleaning. (prohibition)

- As you see in the chart, *could have* is used with possibility. It can also be used in another, more subtle context: *a possibility that was not acted on* (a missed opportunity).

    Mina was late for class. She could have overslept. (It's possible the reason she was late is that she overslept; we don't know for sure).

    Mina was late for class. She could have asked me for a ride. (Mina had the option to ask for a ride, but she didn't, so she was late.)

Grammar Summary **161**

Review of Passive Voice

simple present	The animals **are** kept in tiny cages. It's cruel.
simple past	Dogs _____ _____ 15,000 years ago.
present perfect	They _____ _____ **trained** to do police and rescue work.
present continuous past continuous	The lost cat **is / was** _____ **cared for** by a volunteer at the animal shelter.
simple future	The cat _____ **be** _____ to its owner tomorrow.
with modals	Parrots **can** be taught to communicate with humans. Dogs **should** _____ _____ on a leash.

❶ Forming the passive: Use a form of be + the past participle. With modals: modal + be + past participle

❷ To show who does the action, use by + noun: *The lost cat* **was found** *by a neighbor.* If it's clear who does the action, or if it's not important, don't use by + noun: *Parrots* **can be taught** *to speak.*

❸ You might use the passive if:
- It's obvious who did something or the doer of the action is a general group of people: *Parrots can be taught to speak.* (We know humans are the ones teaching.)
- The action is more important than who does it: *The boy was bitten by a spider.*

- Remember, when you change a sentence from active voice to passive voice, the pronoun changes from an object pronoun to a subject pronoun.

   My friends gave **me** *a puppy for my birthday.*
   I *was given a puppy for my birthday.*

The Conditional

1. With possible (real) future events		2. With imaginary (unreal) present situations	
if *clause*	*result clause*	if *clause*	*result clause*
If I **do** that,	I'll **have** enough money	If you **had** a scholarship,	you **would have** enough money,

❶ This form of the conditional is used to make predictions and talk about possible future events. The verb in the *if* clause is in the <u>simple present</u>. In the result clause, the verb is in the <u>simple future</u>.

❷ This form of the conditional is used to talk about imaginary present events. The information in the *if* clause is not true right now. The result clause describes an imagined result. The verb in the *if* clause is in the <u>simple past</u>. In the result clause, *would(n't)* + verb is used. Note: be ⟶ were for all subjects in the *if* clause: If I / you / he <u>were</u> the teacher . . .

Phrasal Verbs

A phrasal verb is a verb + preposition/particle. Some phrasal verbs are "separable;" the verb can be "separated" from the preposition/particle by an object (noun or a pronoun). Notice the placement of the pronoun in the separable verbs. Phrasal verbs have different meanings than the base verb on its own, as you will see in Activity **A**.

	With an object	Without an object
separable	She **gave up** her job. / She **gave** her job **up**. ~~She gave up it.~~ / She **gave** it **up**. Other examples: *put off, size up, think over*	She **bounced back** (recovered) from her illness. The plane **took off** on a dangerous mission. Other examples: *die down, pick up, step in*
inseparable	She **looked after** her colleagues. The doctor **looked after** them. Other examples: *find out, put up with*	

> Some phrasal verbs have three words. They are always inseparable: *How much longer do we have to* **put up with** *this rain? / Every winter I* **come down with** *a cold.*

- Phrasal verbs, like regular verbs can have more than one meaning. Some phrasal verbs can be used both transitively and intransitively.

  take off

  The plane eventually took off. (It left the ground.)

  Her career is really taking off. (It's going well.)

  He won't take his hat off. (He won't remove it.)

  I took three weeks off last summer. (I had a vacation.)

Reported Speech

> **Notice!** Some verbs (*convince, remind, tell*) can follow more than one pattern.

Use reported speech to explain what someone else has said. The verb tense, certain time words (such as *now, last week*), and pronouns can shift in reported speech.

Patterns in reported speech:

❶ verb + (*that*) clause: Ana **said (that) she was taking a kickboxing class.**
   use with verbs: *explain, insist, mention, say*

❷ verb + pronoun/noun + (*that*) clause: Derek **told me (that) he played rugby.**
   use with verbs: *convince, promise, remind, tell*

❸ verb + pronoun/noun + infinitive: Derek **encouraged his team to practice** more.
   use with verbs: *beg, convince, encourage, invite, remind, tell*

> **Notice!** Pattern 3 verbs are often used to ask for something or to give advice or instructions.

Grammar Summary

Skills Index

Credits

Photo Credits

Unit 1   pp.x–1, top left: hfng/Shutterstock.com; top right: ©iStockphoto.com/Aldo Murillo; bottom left: Dynamic Graphics/Thinkstock; bottom right: ©iStockphoto.com/Daniel Laflor; **p.2**: Mike Theiss/National Geographic Stock; **p.3**: Yuri Arcurs/Shutterstock.com; **p.4**: Niagara705/Dreamstime.com; **p.5**: Bojana/Shutterstock.com; **p.6**: National Geographic Maps/National Geographic Image Collection; **p.6–7**: Kenneth Garrett/Getty Images; **p.9**: beltsazar/Shutterstock.com; **p.10**: Frans Lanting/National Geographic Stock

Unit 2   pp.12–13: Freesurf69/Dreamstime.com; **p.14**, left: ©iStockphoto.com/Gorfer; right (top): Frans Lanting/National Geographic Stock; right (bottom): Unfetteredmind/Dreamstime.com; **p.15**, left: Celsopupo/Dreamstime.com; right: Leire Unzueta/National Geographic Stock; **p.16**, top: zhangyang13576997233/Shutterstock.com; **p.17**: zimmytws/Shutterstock.com; **p.18**, top: Helga Esteb/Shutterstock.com; bottom: Panoramic Images/National Geographic Stock; **p.19**: Frans Lanting/National Geographic Stock; **p.20**: Kenneth Garrett/National Geographic Stock; **p.21**, top: Robodread/Dreamstime.com; **p.22**: Tupungato/Shutterstock.com

Unit 3   pp.24–25: Jim Richardson/National Geographic Stock; **p.26**: Andy Z./Shutterstock.com; **p.28**, left to right: Goodluz/Shutterstock.com; Blend Images/Alamy; Andresr/Shutterstock.com; **p.29**: Jim Richardson/National Geographic Stock; **pp.30–31**: Michael Melford/National Geographic Stock; **p.32**: Jim West/Alamy; **p.33**: Seif1958/Dreamstime.com; **p.34**: Radu Razvan/Shutterstock.com

Unit 4   pp.36–37: Hugh Sitton/Corbis; **p.38**, top: Getty Images; top inset: Roy van Ingen; bottom: Dwphotos/Dreamstime.com; **p.40**: Scott Mitchell/ZUMA Press/Corbis; **p.41**, top: Featureflash/Shutterstock.com; bottom: Jack.Q/Shutterstock.com; **p.42**, top: Kaarsten/Dreamstime.com; bottom, Hemis/Alamy; **p.43**: David Alan Harvey/National Geographic Stock; **p.44**, top: Arunas Gabalis/Shutterstock.com; middle: Lebrecht Music and Arts Photo Library/Alamy; bottom: Chris Hill/National Geographic Stock; **p.46**: Karramba Production/Shutterstock.com; **p.47**: Cristian Nitu/Dreamstime.com

Unit 5   pp.48–49: Joel Sartore/National Geographic Stock; **p.50**, left: Getty Images; right: AFP/Getty Images; **p.51**: StockShot/Alamy; **p.52**: Yuri Arcurs/Shutterstock.com; **p.53**: Konstantin Yolshin/Shutterstock.com; **p.55**: THP/Tim Hester Photography/Shutterstock.com; **p.56**: Bobby Model/National Geographic Stock; **p.57**: George F. Mobley/National Geographic Stock; **p.58**: Mike Parry/Minden Pictures; **p.59**: JG Photography/Alamy

Unit 6   pp.60-61: PictureNet/Corbis; **p.62**, top: MBI/Alamy; bottom: Art Kowalsky/Alamy; **p.64**, top: Mark Seberini/Dreamstime.com; bottom: Edwin Verin/Dreamstime.com; **p.65**: Camilla Watson/Getty Images; **p.66**: John Kasawa/Dreamstime.com; **p.67**, top: Andrey Burmakin/Shutterstock.com; bottom: Andresr/Shutterstock.com; **p.68**: VideojugBeauty/YouTube; **p.69**: conrado/Shutterstock.com; **pp.70-71**: Stephen Bisgrove/Alamy

Unit 7   pp.72–73: Tino Soriano/National Geographic Stock; **p.74**, top: Mika Heittola/Shutterstock.com; bottom: Ira Block/National Geographic Stock; **p.76**: Yusef El-Mansouri/Shutterstock.com; **p.78**, top: Rohan Van Twest/Alamy; bottom left: Supri Suharjoto/Shutterstock.com; bottom right: Kzenon/Shutterstock.com; **p.80**: ©iStockphoto.com/Henrik Jonsson; **p.81**: Morgan Lane Photography/Shutterstock.com; **p.82**: Katrina Brown/Dreamstime.com; **p.83**: David Cupp/National Geographic Stock

Unit 8   pp.84–85: Keith Barraclough/National Geographic Stock; **p.86**: Dirk Anschütz/Corbis; **p.87**: Mike Theiss/National Geographic Stock; **p.88**, top: William Weems/National Geographic Stock; bottom: Catalin Petolea/Shutterstock.com; **p.89**: Mika/Corbis; **p.93**, top: Image Source/Corbis; bottom: Dmytro Konstantynov/Dreamstime.com; **p. 94**, top: Cristi_m/Dreamstime.com; middle: Benoit Tessier/Reuters/Corbis; bottom: StockLite/Shutterstock.com; **p.95**, left: Caro/Alamy; right: Ianni Dimitrov/Alamy

Unit 9   pp.96–97: Patrick Shyu/National Geographic Stock; **p.98**: Jmiks/Shutterstock.com; **p.100**, top: Richard Laschon/Shutterstock.com; middle: donatas1205/Shutterstock.com; bottom: Vincent J. Musi/National Geographic Stock; **p.101**: John Elk III/Alamy; **p.102**: Gary Roberts/Alamy; **p.103**: Michael Nichols/National Geographic Stock; **p.105**, top: Konrad Wothe/Minden Pictures; middle: Medford Taylor/National Geographic Stock; bottom: Shawnjackson/Dreamstime.com; **p.106**: Renate Micallef/Dreamstime.com; **p.107**: Picsfive/Shutterstock.com

Unit 10   pp.108–109: Jim Richardson/National Geographic Stock; **p.110**, left (top): Gelpi/Shutterstock.com; (bottom): Chris Rout/Alamy; right: Peter Zoeller/Design Pics/Corbis; **p.111**: Sandra Eckhardt/Corbis; **p.113**: James Woodson/Thinkstock; **p.114**: takito/Shutterstock.com; **p.115**: Chris Crisman/Corbis; **p.116**: auremar/Shutterstock.com; **p.117**: MedusArt/Shutterstock.com; **p.118**: Nik Wheeler/Corbis

Unit 11   pp.120–121: Sigurdur Hrafn Stefnisson; **p.122**, top: Reuters/Corbis; bottom: George F. Mobley/National Geographic Stock; **p.123**: AFP/Getty Images; **p.124**: John Lund/Drew Kelly/Blend Images/Corbis; **p.125**, left to right: Jack Reynolds/Getty Images; Brian Thompson/National Geographic Stock; Mike Theiss/National Geographic Stock; **p.126**, top: Czacio/Dreamstime.com; bottom: John Wollwerth/Dreamstime.com; **p.127**: Chris Collins/Corbis; **p.128**: Kristina Afanasyeva/Dreamstime.com; **p.129**: Jim Reed/Jim Reed Photography - Severe & /Corbis; **p.130**: Sam Kittner/National Geographic Stock

Unit 12   pp.132–133: Chuck Pefley/Alamy; **p.134**, top: Jonathan Larsen/Diadem Images/Alamy; bottom: Jason Swalwell/Shutterstock.com; **p.135**: Shelly Castellano/Icon SMI/Corbis; **p.136**, top: Vico Collective/Alin Dragulin/Blend Images/Corbis; bottom: new vave/Shutterstock.com; **p.137**: Seandnad/Dreamstime.com; **pp.138–139**: Fritz Hoffmann/National Geographic Stock; **p.139**: John Warburton-Lee Photography/Alamy; **p.140**: Ang Wee Heng John/Dreamstime.com; **p.141**. Myrleen Pearson/Alamy; **p.143**: Ben Radford/Corbis

Text Credits

Readings from the following units were adapted from National Geographic.

Unit 1 Adapted from *Searching for Cleopatra* by various, National Geographic Extreme Explorer, January/February 2011. **Unit 2** Adapted from *Traveling Troubadour* by Keith Bellows, *National Geographic Traveler,* March 2011. **Unit 3** Adapted from *Plugging into the Sun* by George Johnson, National Geographic Magazine, September 2009. **Unit 4** Adapted from *Hip-Hop Planet* by James McBride, National Geographic Magazine, April 2007 **Unit 7** Adapted from *Changing America* by Joel L. Swerdlow, National Geographic Magazine, September 2001 **Unit 9** Adapted from *Orphans No More* by Charles Siebert, National Geographic Online, September 2011. **Unit 10** Adapted from *Beautiful Brains* by David Dobbs, National Geographic Magazine, October 2011. **Unit 12** Adapted from *Battle for the Soul of Kung Fu* by Peter Gwin, National Geographic Magazine, March 2011.